TIFFANY KORY

Mr.
Mrs.
Ms.
Miss.
Me.

NO MATTER THE TITLE, RISE FROM TRAUMA TO TRIUMPH AND LEARN TO LOVE YOURSELF.

Cover design by DG Marco Alvarez
Layout by Manuel Serna

For more information, contact:
Fig Factor Media I www.figfactormedia.com
Blushing Royalty, LLC

Printed in the United States of America

ISBN: 978-1-952779-65-7
Library of Congress Control Number: 2021912664

Ms.

No Matter the Title, Rise from
Trauma To Triumph and Learn to
Love Yourself.

Contents

Acknowledgements

I would like to thank all my amazing angels who helped me make this dream a reality, but especially a few;

My parents and sister, who felt this with me and were always there to talk any time. Any day.

My salon clients, teachers, and friends who supported me and listened to me when I was so scared to get up.

Becky, for the referral that day when I was feeling discouraged at the grocery store and you called to get me to take action on publishing my book.

Jacqueline, Gaby, and Michele, (Fig Factor Media), I needed you so much throughout this process and it meant so much to me to have people who are not only experts and extremely talented, but also that I can be open with and trust to keep going, even when I doubted myself or was scared of telling my story.

Lauren for always believing in me, helping me, and listening.

Tam, Robbie, and all my friends who listened to my fears and told me to go for my dreams anyways.

Shirin for encouraging me to go back to school and being my other half in this journey. I will always want the absolute best for you, too.

Becky for teaching me how to date and be smarter and that I am worth nothing less than the best. You are also so strong, and you motivate me to be better. (You are kind, you are beautiful, you are special, you are intelligent, you are important...I love you).

Candace for being my sister who oh so gracefully tells me when I am wrong and guides me to live life happily and to the fullest. Yet, always wiped my tears and held me when I felt the most agonizing loneliness.

Annie for reminding me of what the scriptures say. Always there to listen and make me smile and tell me words of affirmation.

To my precious son, if it weren't for your kindness, kisses, words of encouragement, and extremely positive attitude, I don't know where or what I would be doing. You are my prince and everything I do in my world is for you. Always chase your crazy dreams and never ever let anyone tell you cannot do something. Stand up for yourself and do not keep it bottled inside. If I could grow wings, I would fly you anywhere you want to go. I love you more than the moon.

Love, Mama

Introduction

We all want the future to hold big promises, abundant wishes and fulfilled dreams. Sometimes I ask why things have to be so difficult for some and easier for others, but I do not question my why. I certainly relish in the ideals of a perfect marriage, but I wouldn't be the woman I am today, if I complained that marriage isn't always perfect. Marriage to my ex-husband was a huge disappointment for me, but I learned not to give up on being my best self through adversity. I like to think that I rose to the occasion and believed in having a great marriage, no matter the obstacles. For those who go through trauma, having self-empowerment really makes one unique and special, which is key to finding love for yourself again. I'm still rising, above-it-all, post-divorce with inner strength in navigating the maze of being divorced and having the life I deserve for myself and my child.

I will never forget my hope and faith in working hard to combat relationship misery with courage and bravery in accepting the road I've been on, finding what really matters to me and knowing there is indeed triumph for perseverance, for which I am thankful for. Having gratitude is so important in the midst of adversity, as I've learned gratitude is empowering.

As I continue down my persevering path in these

ever-changing, sometimes daunting times, even if I feel loneliness, I am excited about my place and the time that I am in, today. My overall well-being is my challenge, not my former life, where my beauty, strength, wellness, intelligence, and core were all jeopardized as once a wife, holding so much disillusionment and sadness, fight and flight anxiety, and determination every day thereafter, post-divorce. I reflect on where I've been and how far I have come since being raised in Georgia along the pecan orchards and smell of sweet peaches and magnolias, with good family values and landing in the faster paced Illinoian competitive Midwest, rising up, making a life for myself that hasn't come easy for me. The fact that I can take pride in, as a Ms., with newfound higher standards for myself and my son, is something I embrace, in creating my new identity where I can stand tall, as a Ms. in sharing what I have experienced and learned from by stepping down a victorious path. Nowadays, I have so much at my fingertips because of my choices, what I don't settle for, and what I chose to part with and accept for the better. Living out my dream as a single mother having gone through emotional and verbal abuse trauma to then feel triumphant in my own life is exhilarating. I am a 40-year-old mother to an adorably perfect and gentle-hearted son, who is proud to call me Mama even while he is on leave with his father, which is my loneliest time. I am working ambitiously in taking my status of being a Ms. all the way to new heights as an entrepreneur and pageant queen showing my best-heeled foot forward, holding onto hope that there is no impossibility in our future.

In my entire being, my authentic and courageous story I share, is about having my faith, being self-reliant, independent and dignified in picking up the pieces behind me and finding new starts, even when I feel knocked down. However, as much as I try to stay optimistic on my course, I know my dreams will come to fruition, as a mother whose son will look up to and learn from in seeing a good world through my lens. Being a Ms. is a positive title, whether I am at the grocery store or bank, to being just me at home as a doting single mother, running my businesses, writing or painting or planning for a charity, to a runway donning a sash and crown or on the dating scene to find the true love in my future soulmate. I thrive to surpass every expectation.

This is my story of empowerment in helping others see that they can absolutely change their course, like the color of their hair! Transforming oneself comes first in finding a source of inner power to shine outwardly in healing from domestic abuse, which is verbal, emotional or physical trauma. I am elated to share all that is in store for those who have one foot out the door, fellow divorcee's and single mothers who could use the motivation, encouragement, and the light of my meaningful pageant crown to cast hope for bigger and better times ahead.

This book was written for those lives in need of having a creative mind, moving thoughts and vision of thinking outside of the box for what could and can be and building the willpower of investment in choices and options for a better place for any woman in any circumstance. Seeing and believing once the tears are wiped away, and the storms that make you hold onto your faith scatter, bringing rainbows of hope and healing.

This memoir is a shadow of my life that follows me everywhere with silver linings and lessons of the heart that help me be a whole person again and a lot stronger than I would ever have thought of being and imagined needing to be, without my faith. Always have hope for tomorrow, without hope, there is fear. I have goals such as revisiting my love for horse life, as I write my first of many true and relatable stories, please join me for a ride through the fields of glory learning to be a friend to yourself. Make goals, put your self-care first, be strong in the days that never resist in raising children without fear in doing it on your own, as a co-parent and 100% as a thriving mother. In order to feel good about myself, out of divorce, I choose each day to be a vision of beauty inwardly finding my beauty again, out of the darkness of divorcing that once roadblocked my every move and channeling my innate energy to do goodwill in giving back by utilizing my platform, spreading the pageant love as a role model and sharing personal joys. With goodness from the heart and my son's precious involvement, I am paving a way to serve others through my skills and talents in being success driven.

The notion "Heavy is the head that wears the crown," (originally by William Shakespeare), comes to mind, while there is a way to have post-divorce success out of a marriage gone awry, I sincerely believe that I have Angels on Earth who have been by my side helping me along my unraveled, imperfect road, with whom have seen me at my worst and also in my best light and have rooted for me along the way. I am fortunate to have such a support group picking up relationships and friendships that have held my stability and growth in the forefront. I am grateful to share my memoir to keep on rising up through my personal challenges even further, discovering bountiful blessings for myself and wishing everything for others' lives who take from my message of hope and healing out of trauma to triumph. Everything I have is because of the dismantling of a dysfunctional relationship that happened for only one good reason...my son. My son is going to grow into a man who knows differently and that is the most important effort in changing the tides in time and I believe, this is my purpose in life.

Dedication

This book, I dedicate to my son, for which someday he will look back and know that there is a different reward to a fulfilling love and marriage. I have high hopes that he will apply the good qualities, the healthy characteristics of interpersonal communications in every relationship he has, whether in casual friendships or in marriage. My hopes are for him to form his own triumphant love in having his own happy family and raise his children with love and break the cycle of divorce and the statistics surrounding children of divorce.

- *35% of children of divorce will experience their own divorces someday*

- *50% of all children in the United States of America will witness the end of a parent's marriage*

- *50% will most likely marry another partner who was a child of divorce once before*

- *Children are more likely to experience developmental and social behavior issues when parents divorce when the child is between the ages of 7 to 14*

- *There is a 16% increase in behavioral and emotional problems in this age range especially*

- *Children of divorce are found to be two times more likely to commit suicide, four times likely to have mental problems and social issues, 300% more likely to experience mental health issues and have a greater risk for cancer and poverty*

The statistics and research are according to the (CDC, Verywell family, census.gov, The Guardian, Survive Divorce Marripedia, Marriage Success Secrets, Center for Social Justice, MDRC), Authored by Maria Lazic. This 2021 report: 13 Saddening Children of Divorce Statistics for 2021 journal includes the following notable statistics:

- 73% of divorces happen because of lack of commitment
- 56% of divorces take place because of arguing too much
- 55% of divorce is in result of cheating
- 25% of divorce are abusive relationships.

Furthermore, in 2017, a study found that children living in intact, nuclear families are about half as likely as children in step, blended, or one parent families to have a mental disorder or need psychological help. Also, many adult children of divorce may be vulnerable to drug and alcohol abuse in adolescence, have fears about commitment and divorce, and have negative memories of the legal system that forced custody and visitation per key "Statistics about Kids from Divorced Families" by Journalist Wayne Parker. One key point the author points out is that regardless of the reason for divorce, parents should reassure their children that they aren't losing their parents, even though a marriage is dissolving. Also, most importantly, have hopes that many children of divorce fare better off after a divorce, especially when a divorce removes them from a high conflict situation that involves abuse.

As a divorcee, I am shocked by statistics surrounding children of divorce and feel compelled to make changes for the betterment of my son's growing years by depending on professional help in being a proactive and prepared single mother/parent. The statistics, research and need for support in divorce is staggering, in my opinion.

Where do I begin? I will start by telling you that yes, "you", you didn't deserve this pain. You don't realize it now, but the heartbreak, the pain, the screaming cries that brought you to your knees, the inability to get your head out from under the covers, it had to happen to get you to MOVE! You are a generational curse breaker. Breaking the cycles of trauma whether it is post-divorce trauma stress disorder or everyday stress and distress in a marriage *that is troubled, God knew when he created you that you had the power to break the cycle of a bad marriage, by changing your last name and finding out essentially, what your name represents for yourself, to others and possibly even your child(ren). Your pain is your purpose. Just like trauma can happen at any moment...miracles can too.*

This is not a book that encourages anyone to get divorced. Rather, I want to prevent you from making mistakes that lead to bigger problems later, and, if you are going through heartbreak from a breakup, help you to not feel alone. Because, girlfriend, I've been there. You feel like you have nobody. Nobody to hug you, support you, celebrate with you, listen to you, or maybe just to love you. But the reality is, you are not alone. You've got the most important person in the world in your corner: you!

When I was a young girl, my parents taught me hard work and independence. My stepdad would make us do yard work, mow the lawn, build a deck, change tires and I threw fits and cried the whole time. I said to him "one day I will find a husband who doesn't LET me do any of these things." Yeah, I found him all right. With that, I lost my independence. He took over my finances; he was the decision maker. He influenced the color of my hair and nails, what I wore, and made sure every minute of the day I was doing what he told me to do, or what I should be doing better. I was given an unlimited allowance and never had to lift a finger around the house (the hard stuff). Everything appeared to be perfect from the outside. Until one day, he didn't want me anymore. I had no control. However, after being forced to take it back (hello, in the face of trauma, your inner Ms. is a fierce champion!), I, finally, became a Queen of Independence.

Here is my story. How I gained the title of Ms. (Illinois and hopefully Ms. World/Universe/USA one day) on my runway of life. I want to help you discover the titanium power of the Ms. title inside you, walk life's ultimate stage from trauma to triumph with you and rise above adversity through the journey of self-love so you, too, can take the title you've deserved all along. No contest.

Preface

NJ Kory is the nine-year-old son of Tiffany Kory. NJ is one of Tiffany's biggest supporters and has been there every step of the way. He has watched as she has transformed herself from just his mom to Ms. Illinois World International 2021 and now as she follows her path to authorship. At just nine years old, NJ shares how his mom's career has helped him understand the importance of staying true to himself, forging strong relationships, and giving back to others.

Tell us about yourself and your family NJ?

Hello, my name is NJ, and cats are probably my favorite animal. My parents are divorced, and I have to switch from house to house to house to house. So, it's sometimes hard doing that. I'm also an only child, and I don't have any brothers or sisters. I have cousins but, my cat Lily, is kind of like my sister.

What would you tell someone else who has parents who are divorced?

That it's still okay that your parents are divorced, it can also be fun sometimes because you get two Christmases, and you get two birthdays. That is the fun thing about your parents being divorced. I also play the electric guitar, and I like having two guitars at my dad's and my mom's. I love playing with both of them, and I can always practice at their houses.

I would also say that at both houses you can still make friends if you try to. When you are nice to others, you can make really good friends. They'll probably be your best friends forever.

What's the best part of spending time with mom? Can you share something that your mom maybe did for you that just made you feel special?

She's always laughing. She's fun. She's encouraging, and she likes doing stuff with me. Oh, and that she always has people over that I can play with. She also does my hair, and she sometimes dyes my hair blue, which I actually love that she does. Not too long ago, I even got a mohawk!

I've had a ton of good times with her, but I think my favorite was probably when we went to Six Flags on Halloween. We got to see the people getting their makeup done for Cosmetology day. We also saw the parade, and after the parade, we were walking around, and we were getting scared from every end, and there were scary things everywhere. It was a scary time but really fun!

What's your favorite thing to do in your free time?

In my free time, I either like to go down to my friend's house, or I like playing with my friends, grinding on games, because I'm making memories I'm probably going to keep forever. Another thing I like playing is my VR headset so that I can be social with other people that way too. I do Tik Tok too, and I mostly like to do Roblox.

What was it like watching your mom compete?

I think my favorite part was when she won, and I got to see her being crowned. I legit just got up, and I was clapping. I had my fingers crossed for her, and I was hoping that she would win, and it happened. She won. I had so much fun being there!

How do you help your mom? What do you tell her about competing?

When she's down, I say, "Well, at least you have me because I'm always here for you," and if she doesn't win, I say, "Never give up, keep on trying until you accomplish it!" She also has a stuffed animal named Marshmallow. Because her favorite candies are Reese's, I would probably give her some Reese's and Marshmallow.

What do you think about charity and being able to share your gifts and talents with others? How has your mom inspired you to do this?

Charity is about giving, not taking, not stealing, and not any bad things. I've done a ton of charities with my mom. And I always liked doing that with her when she had those types of events.

I like seeing the smiles on people's faces when they get their stuff. I feel like they deserve to have food and don't deserve to be treated badly because they lost their jobs. No one deserves to have that.

Do you think that some of the work that she's been doing has inspired you to better yourself?

Yes, I'm in total agreement with that because she has taught me to be myself. And now that I'm myself now, I try to do things that other people might not. I try things that sometimes can be gross, spicy, and weird.

What do you think is the most important quality that your mom should look for in dating?

Oh my gosh, I've said things about her dating other men a ton of times. I think that, like celebrities, my mom is hard to get married to. She has to find the right man. She handles relationships, a-okay sometimes. But I don't think the men handle the relationship with her. I usually know if it's the right man for mom or if it's not. I would also want him to be nice to me.

What do you imagine your mom's career to look like in ten years?

Oh boy. So, I would expect her to keep on doing makeup and hair because she's amazing at it. And once she gets a ton of money, she can retire, and she's fine for life. She could probably even build a whole building, so she will still make money when she is retired. If she retires, I'll be proud of her for making enough money out of her books and her skincare line.

What about for yourself, what do you think you'll be doing ten years from now?

It would be my dream to be famous on YouTube. So, I'll probably make a YouTube channel. You have to be thirteen to do YouTube, so I have a couple of years until that happens. I think with my guitar, I'll even try to make an intro and then an outro for my YouTube videos.

What do you think your mom means by the saying "a queen doesn't need a king"? What does that mean for you?

I think that means it's sometimes okay to be alone. You can have some fun sometimes even being lonely, like meeting new people. I've met a ton of people, and then I'm like, "Oh. They're my best friends forever now."

What do you have to say to your mom, and why do you think people should read her book?

I want to say good luck! I hope that everyone learns the lesson from her book and that they should really read it to know that a queen doesn't need to have a king and that it's okay being alone sometimes.

No one's perfect. Never give up and keep on trying until you accomplish that goal of getting Ms. World or graduating from something. Because she never gave up on graduating from Cosmetology school and pageants. She did amazing there. So, accomplish your goals, and never give up.

NJ hopes that by sharing his experiences with his family and his trusty companion and cat, Lily, he has helped you understand what he has learned about having Ms. Illinois World International 2021 as his mom.

PART 1:

"MISS"

Prepare for love.

GROWING UP A GEORGIA PEACH

I grew up in a little town called Perry, GA. I had the most wonderful childhood. I had a loving family, and everything was amazing. My stepdad was and is my dad, so when I refer to my dad I am talking about him, (not the coward who wanted nothing to do with my sister and I). My mom remarried after my biological father cheated on her when I was only two, so I didn't know the difference because he was my dad. He had two older sons and my mom had my older sister, and I was the baby of the whole gang. My mother was talented, beautiful, loving and supportive. My dad was hard working, loving, kind, and caring. He was at all our games and practices that he could attend. He taught us how to do everything and even though we hated his stewed tomatoes, he took great care of us. Family isn't always necessarily blood. They love you unconditionally. UNCONDITIONALLY. No matter what you do, they love you. To my amazing stepdad, I was his little princess, sticking my tongue out and giggling along the way.

I had a great Christian upbringing. I learned honesty, kindness, grace, forgiveness, and I always have and will love Jesus. Georgia is always going to be "home." I had the most amazing friends and neighbors. We lived by a lake and my friends had boats, four wheelers, and jet skis. We had docks to fish from and built swings we made of trees and played all day, every day. We slept on the trampoline and repeated. Our neighbors were all friends, and my favorite memories were Fourth of July parties on the lake. My best friends down the lake, they were brother and sister, and they had loving and awesome parents and cousins. We did everything together. Often in the evenings, the dads would spend all their time chatting around the BBQ'd meat they hunted earlier with their sons and dogs. The beautiful Southern mamas would be laughing and cheering as the kids all sitting on the dock eating would get sprayed by a random jet ski rider. I was so happy every single day.

At school, I was a cheerleader. I played softball, took

art lessons, and did English horseback riding across the street from my house at a beautiful Kentucky-style farm. I had two horses I was responsible for. Corora was all white and Bonecca was a solid warm brown beauty. They were kind and calm. Strong and graceful. My teacher was amazing, and I was so happy riding through trails and trees with them on days we were allowed to after training hard. I bathed them and brushed them and took the best care of them. This was when I fell in love with horses.

One day, when I was fourteen years old, my mom and dad sat us down and gave us the news that we are moving to Illinois because of my dad's work. It wasn't so bad for me, but for my big sister it was more difficult. She was sixteen, first chair concert cellist and number one on the tennis team. She had a boyfriend she had to say goodbye to. My heart was broken for how hard it was on her, so I just went with the flow and trusted my parents that we would be okay.

My dad still would have us doing a lot of chores and work around the new house. It was a big house in a nice neighborhood surrounded by trees and had a reputation of being the nicest neighborhood in town. I had no problem making friends very quickly. I was still required to help out around the house. I had to mow the lawn and even helped my dad build an unbelievable two-story deck. I would complain and throw fits all along the way. One day, he even had me change all four tires from one car to switch with another car before I could go "hang out" with friends. He is a huge NASCAR fan and I felt like I was being timed like the pit crew! As a teenager, I would sass back to him saying, "One day I will find a husband who doesn't LET me do this work!" He would laugh and say, "Be careful what you wish for. Keep going and there will be more work for you to do when this is done." He worked hard and provided a wonderful life for our family. My mom worked hard too as a chef on the local news and opened a shop in the downtown area where she showed her decorating and cooking talents, and everyone loved her. She was warm, beautiful, kind, and extremely talented.

Illinois was much different than Georgia. It was completely flat, and we lived in the middle of the cornfields. It was a smaller town with only 5,000 people and the factory my dad managed was there and the two other factories that made the town survive made the whole town smell like burnt corn and syrup. There was a lake in nearby Decatur, but everyone said, "Don't ever swim in there or you will grow an eleventh toe!"

Everyone was in such a hurry and not as warm and relaxed. When we moved in, my mom went across the street to introduce herself to a new neighbor and the woman turned around after she saw my mom coming and ran into her house and closed the garage door in her face!

Growing up in the South we would welcome neighbors with food for weeks and post a note of where to return the plates which meant they had to come visit us and become friends. Needless to say, it was different, but I maintained a positive attitude.

Softball was fast pitch and that was not easy for me since I was used to slow pitch, but I made friends that way. I tried basketball and I mostly just hated shorts that came down to my knees. When I accidentally scored for the other team because nobody told me you're supposed to switch sides of the court at half-time, I was screamed at so badly by the dads that my mom let me quit. I tried horseback riding and all they had was Western riding, not my pretty English. I tried to learn how to rope barrels instead of jumping fences, but my horse, Lady, almost killed me a few times and it started scaring me terribly, so I eventually quit. And it snowed here! Like, real, white, sledding and school cancellation snow! That was new and different and became a highlight of the season when school was let out early and we could walk to the local pizza place or ice cream shop with friends after school. My Georgia friends and I still wrote letters back and forth. But I made a few good friends in my new town, and I finished that eighth-grade awkward year.

One of my first days of high school, we got to go to an assembly that changed my whole goal as a teenager.

"Ladies and gentlemen, introducing The Swingsations…!" the principal announced. They were the most amazing group of singers and dancers in bright incredible costumes, and they blew my mind. I said to myself, I WILL be in that. The girls were gorgeous, and the boys were hot! And they could sing?? And be football players and pompon girls and dance like Britney Spears and NSYNC? And the goosebumps all over my whole body from the music made me know this is going to happen to me. I knew I wouldn't settle until I was on that stage.

Working hard and trying out, then eventually, being in that show choir helped me grow very confident and I had a lot going for me. I was awkwardly tall and always hated it. I got teased sometimes and my dad would tell me how one day I will be so glad to be tall. He would tell me people's imperfections were what made them most beautiful. I still remember one time he printed a picture of a face that was a mirrored half of one side of another of a person and how they looked like an alien! I had issues with my teeth from a childhood trampoline accident and I learned to own my not-so-perfect teeth.

My senior year of show choir, we won the National Championship and we got to fly and take a charter bus to places including Chicago, Los Angeles, Nashville, and New York City! The seventy-two boys and girls in the group were like brothers and sisters to me. We toured all over the country and our parents dedicated their whole lives to our rehearsals and creating our costumes and fundraisers, even working at the smoky BINGO hall week after week to raise funds and providing endless amounts of transportation and meals for all our marathon practices and competitions. We learned hard work, teamwork, how to sing, and we had the most talented directors and choreographers in the whole show choir world. Every time we came into town after winning our competitions the whole town showed up like a parade with firetrucks and police and cheering, supportive community members.

I got my first job working in the cornfields "walking beans". It was awful. I made about $5.13 an hour going row by row picking soybeans. In the fields, there were ones with all white flowers and ones with all purple flowers. Our job was to pull the purple ones if we saw them in the white fields and pick the white ones if they were in the purple fields. I remember my parents making me do this job that summer, but they will swear I wanted to because I read that Cindy Crawford did it when she was a teenager. So weird! Why would anyone want to do that!?

The next summer, I got a job working at the huge park district pool as a lifeguard. I loved that job because I loved the children that came to the pool every day in the summer, I learned how to push myself to be an expert at CPR and saving lives, and I looked awesome in a bikini and a tan. The security guards were all super-hot college guys and they began inviting my friends and I to their fraternity parties. Junior and senior year I was balancing thinking I knew it all as a teenager yet starting to cross the line into new things that were exciting, but that I wasn't really supposed to be doing. And I started wearing heels and just like Dad said, I started loving being tall.

What came next was going to change my life and set in motion a life of soul-searching and figuring out things they never teach you how to figure out in school.

BECOMING A YOUNG ADULT

I wasn't always the most well-behaved teenager. There were also issues at home with my sister who still didn't feel like she fit in. She and my parents struggled, and I just started looking at colleges as I was supposed to. I went to orientation for Illinois State University because some of my friends would be going there, too. The first day, at eighteen years old, I met a boy at orientation. Deep breath. He was the most amazing person I had ever laid eyes on. He was laid back, funny, but confident and had a Chicago city-boy swagger about him. What I was most fascinated by was the way he was so respectful and kind to his mother. She was beautiful. She was kind and seemed to like me a lot. As I was alone for the first night in that dorm room calling my best friend from home, strategizing how I could go to a party back at home (forty-five minutes away) and make it back in time for my parents to not find out, I got a knock on the door from the entire baseball team! They invited me down to a room where there was a party. Off I went, hoping that guy was there. He was in the back of the room with girls all around him. I thought, there's no way he would even notice me, but he did! He called me over. We chatted as a group and, eventually, he asked me to go to his room so he could grab his fake ID so we could go get alcohol. (MOM, sorry!!! I went!) He kissed me in the elevator. I melted into a pile of muck on the floor. We went to the liquor store and I was shocked because I had never seen a fake ID before. When we went back to the party he was given the title of "Preview Pimp" from all the guys because, as they said, he got "red shirt and khakis," which was me! We spent the next few days of orientation skipping the classes and sitting under trees making out and sneaking from our parents. I went home and told all the lifeguards at the pool, "I met Mr. Right."

Here's the thing: just because you think you're doing what you're supposed to do, it may not always be that way for the rest of your life and "happily ever after" may not be the end of your story. I have a son and I don't want to say anything bad about his father. My son will figure out his own path. He will make his own choices, and I feel confident I will teach him the value of honesty, hard work, courage, and how to impact others for the greater good.

So, my friend, that leaves you and I and our conversation here. I dedicate my story to you because if you ever feel like you want to look back and remind yourself of who you really are, you must do it as an individual. Alone. From that moment on I never ever was alone. I had that man involved in every decision I ever made from teenager to adult.

Growing up, confidence was not ever an issue for me. I had parents that were loving and supportive and told me every day how smart, beautiful and special I am. Being eighteen, I fell for a guy and I knew he was the man I was going to marry. We had a bright future and never struggled financially. The independent confident girl, however, began to be chipped away from me. I didn't listen to the friends that were trying to warn me. I thought they were just jealous.

THE WORLD WAS MINE

I always worked. But, I was screwing up in college and found myself back at home going to community college and working at a jewelry counter at a department store, missing my friends from ISU, trying to visit my boyfriend every other weekend and crying to just be with my Romeo. He messed up his grades too and his family made him go home to the city and finish away from me because I was a distraction.

One day, while taking links out of a watch, I was approached by a sweet woman who worked in another part of my store. She said, "Young lady, you belong in cosmetics!" I had no idea what that even was. She took me under her wing, even though she was about 4'10" and I was 5'11" we were attached, her arm at my hip. She taught me everything there was to know about makeup and skincare and reminded me to have my nails painted every day, just in case someone wanted to buy the same color as me. She taught me, "'Here ya go" does not mean 'Thank you' and 'Uh huh' does not mean 'You're welcome'". She taught me how to be a saleswoman powerhouse! She also loved me and still is like a grandmother to me to this day. I didn't know at the time that she was an angel sent to me from God.

I loved playing with makeup. I loved studying the ingredients and I knew every angle to take to help women understand why they had to have the whole line and how to use it perfectly at home! I didn't know I was so good at it until after every customer, she would be peeking behind the island in our bay waiting for me to say, "Thank you" and hand them the bag and hug them goodbye and we'd have a mini party the second they walked away! We went to sales meetings and won awards! She taught me to listen, try new things, go for it, and that I could do anything!

I was a makeup artist at a department store and,

eventually, worked my way up to business manager at another high-end department store by ISU, where all my friends were still having fun without me, and I got my first apartment and a pet turtle named Fifi. I later moved in with three other college friends, which I hated because all they did was party. I had work and responsibilities to support myself already. I had to wake up at 5:00 a.m. sometimes to manage my business. They were up until 5:00 a.m. destroying our townhome and being drunk and loud. I worked and worked to the point when I was ready for Chicago. I had to get back closer to my boyfriend! I reached out to and scheduled a meeting with the head regional executive of the cosmetics company I worked for. I drove to, what I then thought was, the biggest mall I had ever seen to meet her in Chicago. Through persistence and showing her my numbers and awards she, finally, said, "How about we put you at the largest cosmetics department in the U.S. and see how you do?"

So, I got a job at Marshall Field's State Street, an iconic department store that, while it is no longer in business, was THE classiest place to shop for decades with its crystal chandeliers and famous Walnut Room for dining. There were over 100 people just in the cosmetics department! They were the best of the best. I was enamored and just found my station and did what I knew. I got an apartment by the train station where my boyfriend told me to live. He got me a kitten and I named her Pishi (Persian for pussycat). I was happy. He was still living at his parents' house trying to graduate from a university, while coming in and out of my adorable apartment. Only three short months later, I was doing so fantastic, they promoted me to business manager on Michigan Ave. I was working on The Magnificent Mile in Chicago by the time I was twenty-three. I lived on my own in a beautiful apartment with my kitten in the suburbs of Chicago taking the train every day.

I was being approached by everyone in the city telling me, "You should be a model". I went to an open casting call at one of the biggest agencies in Chicago. They took me on their runway team and I started doing fashion shows and making extra money on the side modeling! I became a model for Vidal Sassoon and, eventually, they gave the most insane haircut ever for a show. It was a mohawk and I felt like a boy. I wasn't allowed to say anything at those shows, because I was being paid. My boyfriend, however, when I came back to my place crying and showing him my haircut, convinced me to completely quit modeling. Plus, his mother continued to tell me I was too overweight to be a model anyways.

I was with that cosmetics line for four years. I built amazing relationships with my bosses (angels), customers (angels) and my coworkers (angels), and my team (angels). At age twenty-seven, I was offered a promotion with another brand (the biggest brand) to manage ten stores' makeup counters as an account coordinator throughout Chicago and the suburbs. I learned so much in that position. I became the ultimate leader. I was trained in something that not only taught me about how to motivate people based on their age generation, but what makes them tick. My girls and guys were so talented and they always told me as a boss I would never ask of them anything I wasn't willing to try myself. I think they liked it even when I had crazy ideas and they didn't work. I could fail and we could laugh together and keep trying. Plus, I didn't talk to them about what made me motivated, but I asked questions to understand what motivated them. My boss in that role (angel) was and is still a dear friend to me. She taught me to not just WANT to be the next level, but to start BEING it. I was courageous, creative and willing to do anything to achieve big goals for myself and my team. I received the best training and was able to coach and mentor my staff. I was never afraid to do anything. We were all extremely good at sales!

Not everyone was a Tiff lover, though. I had to have thick skin and put up with the drama and the haters. It is not a joke. I, eventually, took a position with another smaller luxurious skincare company as an education executive (territory manager, which my boyfriend reminded me daily was not an executive role) after the economy took a spill and there was talk of my coordinator position being eliminated. I had six states in my territory of every high end department store (such as, Neiman Marcus, Saks Fifth Avenue, Barneys, Bluemercury, and Cosbar). I will never forget the first launch we ever had at a Nordstrom store in the US. I had to train eighty-five incredible cosmetics professionals on Michigan Ave. how to sell serum that retailed for $1,500 a bottle. The science behind it was so revolutionary that the doctor who created it won a Nobel Prize for the main ingredient. The manager there absolutely HATED me. The pressure was on and I went home crying many times so frustrated on how to just get her to like, respect, and support me. I called my counterpart in Georgia (angel) crying about it one evening on my way home from a rough day there and she gave me the best advice that I still use to this day. She said, "Baby, buy her flowers" in her beautiful Southern voice. Flowers? I thought. And I scheduled a meeting with her and while she entered the room ready to punch me in the face, I pulled the flowers out from behind my back and said in my sweetest voice, "This is a peace offering...can we start over?" I had nothing to apologize for, but she didn't know whether to lose it on me or hug me. Eventually, I think she was just so lost for how to be towards me, that she found another victim or fifty. I continued to be successful and grow anyways. Buying flowers for all the haters. What can anyone say about that? "She bought me flowers!"

Four years later, I will have taken a position that came to me by way of someone on Linkedin. I was made an offer

I could not refuse in the salon and spa industry managing the entire Midwest and flying all over the country doing what I loved. My boss, the vice president, Brenda, was, literally, like Kim Catrell from Sex in the City. She was the hottest single grandmother and bad ass woman I had ever seen. She was an angel too, but I didn't know at the time she was the first Ms. I had ever encountered.

HE WAS PERFECT

I dated my boyfriend for nine years. I thought he was my best friend. I didn't sway one time. I would walk down the city streets and in the airports as a strong businesswoman and not be tempted by the men trying to hit on me. I was not a college graduate, however, I made almost six figures and I liked my job. I was respected by many amazing people in the cosmetics industry and I felt like I had a very bright future.

I would ask my boyfriend about marriage and he would say, "You get one ring. I am not going to put a ring on your finger until I can find the biggest, most beautiful ring for it" and I believed it was for the right reasons, not knowing really why. I had pictured the proposal and my wedding since I was a little girl. I was willing to wait until he wanted to do it and just do what I thought I was supposed to do.

What were your dreams of what you wanted for yourself or your wedding when you were little? What was your favorite character from a movie or show that you would dress up as or pretend to be as a child? What was it about that prince charming that made you feel like a princess in your dreams? What did you want to be when you grew up? My favorite Disney movie is Aladdin. I love how Princess Jasmine was told, "You're better seen not heard" then locked in the castle and snuck out, only to find the love of her life for his heart and not his money or title. He also loved her for who she was, not her princess title. I wanted to be taken on a magic carpet ride and have a man grab my hand and say "Do you trust me?" as he shows her "A Whole New World". Girlfriend, do you still have your childhood princess dream?

PART 2:

"MRS."

Love in respect and independence in marriage.

FAIRYTALE WEDDING

I always wanted a destination wedding. My dad was sick, however, and diagnosed with cancer, which he, eventually, fought with everything he had in him and survived. It was just a very scary time for my family. He just wanted to make his baby girl happy and give me what I wanted: my dream wedding. So we decided to get married in Florida, so that we still had the destination, but not out of the country. There were so many fights in the engagement and everyone said it was normal, because it's always just stressful. I remember his one friend saying to him in front of me, "If you ever hurt her..." and thinking how sweet that was and that he just must really like me. Looking back now, I think he just knew who he was and knew he would hurt me.

I remember his dad trying to get him to make me sign a prenup. I didn't want to and I also remember thinking on our wedding day to myself that I couldn't believe I got away with not signing one. I assured him that he was the only man I ever wanted and I would never leave him. When I made a promise to God to love him, cherish him, be loyal to him, honor him in sickness and health, richer or poorer, till death do us part...I meant it.

We were married on the beach in Florida. The resort was like a castle. My flowers were all pinks and whites and greens. My dress was all Swarovski crystals that glistened in the sun. My cake was made to perfection to match the detailed folding and patterns of my dress. My family was all there and everyone had the most amazing time (except my future MIL in her giant poofy black gown). My sister and dad gave the most beautiful speeches. We danced and felt the love. His extended family and mine made me feel like I was growing my family. Off we went to Maui, Hawaii, for our nine day honeymoon under the rainbows. I thought it was magical.

FROM THE BEGINNING

When we came back, he made me cry every single day. He told me I needed to work out more and not "let myself go". I was forced to quit trying modeling ever again, even though I was still being scouted and approached about it all the time. He would say that just because my mom and dad told me I was (pretty, talented, special, smart, could sing, etc.) it didn't make it true. My friends stood up to him. They hated the way he treated me. I spent all my time trying to please him and encourage him. I put him completely before myself. I was a Mrs. and I swore to never be a Ms.

His parents were always financially supportive, but just not loving. I remember one dinner we had with his parents that sticks out in my mind now so significantly. He had just finally graduated from college. His mother looked at his father and said, "He would never be where he is right now if it weren't for you..." and his head went down. I was so angry for them to say that to their son. I picked his chin up off his chest and said, "You can be anything you want to be. You earned that degree. You are so smart and you will be successful because you work hard and you can be whatever you want to be." They were so unbelievably wealthy. They never showed affection to each other and never said, "I love you" or "I am proud of you" or anything.

He had, finally, bought a townhome and I moved in with him before we were married. It was in his name and I didn't care or put any thought into it. I gave him over $1,000 a month and we got a joint savings account that I put a lot of money into. I did the cooking and cleaning as I was told to do. His biggest fights with me were over his porn addiction and that I didn't put his laundry away immediately before hanging out with my neighbors. We went out a lot and I was a well behaved trophy wife.

I was starting to lose control of where our money was going but had to trust my husband and do what I thought I was supposed to do in the steps of life.

MY SON, MY GIFT

My husband, eventually, got into his successful family business and we bought a big house. Then, in the most wonderful way, my world was incredibly changed when I found out I was having a baby. My relationship with my mother-in-law became the absolute worst. I think she was jealous that I was going to be the new "Mama" of the family and the attention was all on me. It went from her being somewhat of my friend to my enemy instantly. She insulted my weight. She insulted my role as a mother. My "mama bear" instincts kicked in immediately. My husband didn't understand. He was still partying and it made me feel completely disgusted, protective, and most of all, trapped.

My due date was Mother's Day...May 7th. However, the little cutie was comfy and didn't want to come out! A week later, I was scheduled to be induced. My baby's birthday was going to be May 14, 2012. It was so great that I was able to time everything to have exactly the OBGYN from my team that I wanted. When I went into labor, my nurse said, "It is time! Where is your husband?" and I realized he told me he was going home to "work out". In the middle of my labor! I was scared and I held onto that nurse. The anesthesiologist came into the room to do the epidural and even though I was afraid, she was one of the most breathtakingly confident and beautiful women I had ever seen. I will never forget that moment with nurse Nancy on a stool in front of me, holding my shoulders and hands and the amazing doctor behind me confidently giving me a needle in my back which I had heard was going to be so painful. My brain was saying, 'WOMAN POWER!' I felt no pain and just laid down and fell asleep. They woke me up to push and my husband was back. An hour and a half later my life was forever changed. He was perfect. I remember when he was born, I took one look at him and it was the first time I felt that level of love. The kind that you can feel as your heart physically grows. After he was born and they let all of the family members come into the room my most incredible nurse Nancy, who helped me through the entire birthing process stayed until everyone left. When she said it was time to take him and let me sleep, she kissed me on the cheek and told me what a great mom I was. She said, "I know which one your mom is". I said, "How?" and she said, "Everyone went directly to the baby. Your Mom went to you because *you* are her baby girl." I love you, Mom.

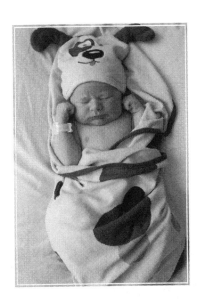

My son was perfect. I was very good at being a mother. I knew that 'coo' meant hungry, 'ca' meant tired and 'wa' meant he wanted his pacifier. My mother-in-law was suffocating me. She wanted to call him "her baby" and it made me sick. She wasn't good at caring for him. She didn't respect me or my routines or even what my doctor was advising me. It was bad. Really bad. My husband backed her up and when they all teamed up against me and made me cry, he would say, "You deserve this".

I want you to know that it is OK to be a good mother. It is OK to be protective and as a mama you do know best. It is OK to feel alone after having a baby and thinking your life changed 110% and everyone else's stayed exactly the same. It is OK to be tired and hormonal. I tell my son now about how I would put him in a bassinet next to my bed so I could keep my hand on his chest at night so I could make sure he was breathing 24/7. You should never be made to feel bad for being a loving, good mother.

TANGLED ROOTS

I hired a nanny and I was traveling every week to different department stores doing training presentations and events and trying to (breast) pump in airport bathrooms and hotels and in the car. Freezing and dating the bags in coolers as much as possible and crying every day because I was tired and being ripped apart for struggling and missing my baby. The more I pumped, the more I would produce and the longer I could provide the benefits of breastmilk to my son. I was also trying to hide in my car and drive and stay away from truckers or cover myself in order to pump while driving, crying and being bitter to my mean mother-in-law who was showing up at my home telling my nanny to go away and trying to take the baby. I didn't mind trying to let her watch him, but this was the most airheaded, physically weak, incompetent person I knew. I would find out about times she showed up and made my nanny leave, while I was in another state being lied to by my husband, and she would be calling my husband to help her because she would get my baby stuck in the high chair or not let him sleep as he was screaming and crying in her care. She wouldn't even give him prescribed medication when he had ear infections or croup and she and my father-in-law went to my pediatrician behind my back as if I was lying that he needed teething medicine (Tylenol or Advil) or had an ear infection. My husband, very wealthy, was busy working with his father and I did what I had to do. I quit my job when my son was four, against my husband's orders. He had so much money and I couldn't understand why he was so obsessed with me bringing in more, I didn't care because no money in the world was going to help my broken mama heart.

I had helped contribute financially for fifteen years of our life together. He would spend money like it was a bottomless pit. We had all the designer clothes and cars and a beautifully furnished home. It looked to the outside world like everything was "perfect". However, I wondered what amount of money would ever satisfy him. I really believe that his insecurity lied with the fact that he was never told, "I'm proud of you", "Good job" or "Thank you" from his parents. He was seeking their satisfaction and I was seeking his.

I felt like he always resented me for being self-made.

In other words, his biggest insecurity was that he looked like a richy-rich boy who had everything handed to him from his father. Yet, he would make it worse by telling everyone how wealthy, smart and amazing he was. I don't think he even knows how to carry on a conversation with another human without bragging about the Rolex his dad got him or the fancy cars he got with daddy's money.

My best friend at the time lived right next door to me and offered me so much support. And yes, when she moved in I took her muffins and we were friends instantly. She had a daughter close to my son's age and we did everything together. We were stroller and wagon-pushing moms of the neighborhood. We went to the zoo, museums, pool, parks, pumpkin patches and so much more every day. It was so wonderful for me to raise my boy. But, with every activity we did I was crying to her because my husband was attacking my every move, even in front of her.

I couldn't understand why a man wouldn't want his wife to raise his baby, especially since we had a lot of money. Isn't it normal for a wife to send cute pictures to her husband at work to show him how happy we were or his milestones? I think I realized later that he was jealous of the love I feel for my son. I am extremely affectionate and maybe he felt like I didn't focus on him enough. I can still hear his footsteps coming up the stairs when I tried to sneak in a nap when the baby napped. He would come home at midday just to shame me for being tired. I wake up in complete terror at the memory of that sound of his shoes coming up the steps, as I would jump up to my feet and pretend to be doing laundry. Anything, just to not be accused of being a complete piece of shit for hours on end. I also will never forget when my son was three years old and we got a letter from the preschool teacher saying he needed help with sharing. It is completely normal for children to learn how to share, especially an only child who never has to at home. As he was in the other room yelling in my crying child's face, "Who do you represent?". I threw everything and ran to my baby's rescue.

The next door neighbors became a really big problem. You know the saying about high fences? (Add to your book list: Caroline Westerhoff's book *Good Fences: The Boundaries of Hospitality*) It's something about getting a bit too close with your neighbors and it definitely didn't matter that they did have a huge fence. I liked my friend being so easily accessible, but there were mornings I would wake up and walk to my coffee maker and her live-in mother was peeking in my patio window saying, "Hello?" and it was chilling! But, we did everything with them. Every weekend the husbands would cook or we would share a babysitter and go out to eat. We did so much together. My friends and family carefully tried to warn me. It was all fine...until it wasn't.

I decided to hop on the Youtube makeup tutorial train. The only place in my huge house I was "allowed" to set up a studio was literally a closet off of the guest room. It was a dark area with no windows and I made it my secret place. I took clients there, even with all the terrible lighting I was allowed to have, and was bringing in a few thousand dollars a month in cash. (Which, I was reminded daily that it wasn't real work or as much money as he made).

I did photoshoots and wedding makeup and private one on ones and sold a direct sales makeup line. My clients and friends were so supportive. Looking back now I am so embarrassed that I had to shove my talents and dreams into a small closet in the huge home. I grew a pretty big following on social media. Blushing Inc. was born, but it was small, and I was scared, overweight, and very sad.

Even at that point in my life when I was the heaviest I had ever been, I still was being asked to get in front of the camera. I tried every diet on the planet. I had a trainer for eight months. I tried eating small amounts of food more often, I tried eating no carbs, shakes, I tried DVDs and running, and weight training. Nothing made me drop one ounce. My mother-in-law calling me fat, my husband calling me fat...the fights we would get in every day over what I was wearing made me start to feel so awful. He would actually cut my clothes. He would scream at me to the point where I was on the floor crying naked and then say, "Now help me pick out what socks I should wear". My babysitters knew. My neighbor/best friend knew. My mother and sister knew because I would call them crying. I didn't know what to do.

I still tried to play the part. I had all the designer handbags and I had makeup parties and a million friends. I made money and it was never acknowledged. I would dress my son in the cutest clothes, and I was trying so hard to just be content.

I could do nothing right, but I was a good mother. My son was perfect and happy. I was living my purpose. I still wanted to make women feel beautiful and I tried to help others out in every way I could.

If you ever feel like you are trying so hard to do what's right and the person you are with isn't supporting you or even being a friend to you, it is okay to be sad. You do not deserve to be punished for doing what feels right in your heart. Their name calling and put downs are a reflection of them, not you. If you put yourself in the position of them and know in your heart that you would never do that to anyone else, it is probably true.

FACING THE TRUTH

When my son was six years old, I started to sense an affair with my next door neighbor, best friend of mine. I could feel it. I was rocking my son to sleep or folding laundry in his front bedroom and I could see them washing cars in the driveways and the way she looked at him and flirted and he flirted back. My husband admitted to me she was making passes at him, touching him when I wasn't looking when we were hanging out. I forbade her from contacting us. I remember every night I was taking my son to the gym so I could take a class and he would go into the childcare room. I would come home and see the other woman that was no longer my best friend look like she was sneaking out my back door crawling home. I told her to stay away from my home and my life and she responded "?". That was the last thing I ever heard from her. I went to the park with my son one night and prayed to God with tears in my eyes to please show me and I remember taking this picture.

I was also walking some evenings with another best friend and neighbor and she was a therapist and gave me so much advice and support (angel). My son was five and about to start kindergarten. She told me to go back to school when my son starts kindergarten. I never finished college and he would always put me down for it, no matter how successful I was or how much money I made. I always wanted to become a cosmetologist, but working I could never make the hours work. Out of nowhere, I found an amazing school close by that was offering a part time program, Monday-Friday 9:00 a.m.-1:00 p.m. It was perfect! I could take my son to school and make it there in time, then even have lunch or a few hours after work, free to get housework done or study before picking him up. I just needed to ask the "boss" and convince him to let me go.

I knew there was something sneaky going on financially. I was at a baby shower of one of my friends and at the large table in front of everyone, one of the other moms said, "Your husband and father-in-law invested a bunch of money with my husband's firm the other day". I said, "What?!" I was mortified. She and all the ladies around the table laughed at me and said, "You didn't know?" I left that shower mortified and came home and asked him. He said, "I can do whatever I want with MY money". So, it was game on.

My radar was up. We started marriage counseling and he just kept saying, "She quit her job without my permission." I think deep down that therapist was trying to tell me with her eyes to leave him. I was so scared, but I knew he was lying to me about where he was all the time. He was trying to convince me to go back to work when my son started Kindergarten. I showed him the beauty school I wanted to attend. He made me do a "presentation" to him while his feet were up on his desk in the office as to why and what I would do with a cosmetology license and I did it. He said no at first and laughed at me. So I told him I was going to just watch Judge Judy every day and do nothing.

I was approached by a dear friend that went to high school with my husband. She was one of the most beautiful women I have ever seen. She was Mrs. Illinois International. She wanted me to compete for her crown. She saw potential in me. I asked my husband and he laughed at me. I inquired about it, anyways. I got all the paperwork and started filling it out.

Eventually, he "let me" go to school two days before it was to start saying, "You're going to need the soft skills" and I ignored it because I was so excited, anyways. My son and I starting school together was amazing as we talked about it and even though I was so nervous, I knew if my son could do the first day of Kindergarten, I could do my first day of beauty school. I remember how we compared what it was like together. He inspired me at thirty-seven years old to go back to school and try my best every day and not be afraid of what will come.

ON MY KNEES

Two weeks into beauty school, I went to the gym with my son. He had swimming lessons and I usually swam beside them so I could still make sure he was safe and get a little exercise myself. We entered the gym and my life forever changed. The sweet girl at the front desk who often babysat for us said, "I saw your husband and ...neighbor/ former best friend...this morning."

I said, "Excuse me?" She said, "They come every morning together". I quickly took my son into his swim lessons and came back to her. She pulled me into an office and printed seven pages of their time punches. For four months every single morning they were meeting inside at the same time, exiting the building and reentering at the same time (minutes) later. As I highlighted and compared the time punches, both of them, 4:37 a.m., 4:41 a.m., 5:02 a.m., 5:17 a.m., and so on every day for four months. She said, "You're shaking, Tiffany". I knew he was an early gym person and he always woke up early to look at porn for as long as I remembered. They were meeting inside, going to his car for maybe two to five minutes of terrible-God knows what, then going back in and working out together!

I came home. My life was flashing before my eyes. I distracted my son and confronted him. He called me crazy at first, of course, then when I showed him the documentation he said, "I haven't loved you since you had a child". I ran to my bathroom and vomited for hours. I couldn't even see. He kept knocking on the door and saying, "Get it together and take care of our son."

I will never ever forget that statement. Looking back now, I think he just wanted me to put our son to bed because he never used to do it and I physically couldn't for the first time in his life.

The next day, I was scheduled to teach a makeup class at Dress For Success in Chicago. I had been volunteering there trying to help the homeless women who they prepared for job interviews to feel their best inside and out. I would donate makeup sample kits with extra money I made from my clients so that they felt polished for their new jobs (label on my makeup kits below). I would meet them individually and teach them how to apply the makeup and take care of their skin, while the staff would help them with clothing and shoes and jewelry and interviewing skills. I wanted them to be fearless and confident also on the outside as the team would help them prepare resumes and mock interview them and we would give them gently used clothes and jewelry for their time entering the workforce. I always felt like I had so much financially, and I had to give back and this was a great opportunity to do that.

I could barely see straight the day I was to present a makeup class to forty high-end women who worked with the charity. I thought I could do it, but minutes before my presentation I ended up curled in a ball in one of the fitting rooms. The director came to me and when I told her I had just caught my husband cheating she couldn't believe I was even there. My two amazing colleagues and friends I had asked to help me were there too, and they sent me home taking care of everything. I ran away and called the "other woman's" husband. I sent him the documents.

Her husband and I had a great friendship. He was kind and loving and a great father and loyal husband and a detective. He and I did things together to bless others secretly and had a great friendship and he believed in God. However, he didn't believe me. He and his wife made it their mission to get the young woman at the gym fired for giving me that information. She knew she was breaking policy and told me she didn't care. I was able to make one phone call and got her a job in cosmetics making much more money. She is an angel too, and to this day says to me, "I would do it again". This beautiful gal is now incredibly successful and shining so bright and I am so thankful for her.

I took my son and escaped to my sister's house. I wonder what she was thinking. I spent five days talking to a lawyer while she made sure my son was OK. Everything was prepared for me to file online. All I had to do was click one button. I was actually, sadly, still in a position that I would have tried to fix things. Sadly, I begged him to talk to me when I was coming home that Sunday. This was the father of my child. He said he wouldn't talk to me until Monday at 1:00 p.m. when I got home from school. I couldn't understand why. I remember calling my mom a lot. She knew everything. She suggested he may be waiting for one more business day to move more money. I had absolutely no idea what our finances really were. I had a lawyer friend draw up the paperwork. I came home that

Sunday night and he was drunk and cooking for me and when I asked for a hug and to talk he pushed me away and said "tomorrow". I went upstairs to my room and called my mom one more time. She said the most perfect words to me, "I will love you and support you no matter what you decide to do." I went online. I filed. I called my mom one more time and she said to me, "Tiffany, nobody fought harder than you to make a toxic marriage work. I am proud of you". I cried myself to sleep.

The next day at 1:00 p.m. I came home from school, and he was sitting there. He said, "Do you want to talk about what you can do better?" I said, "I filed last night. It's over." He said, "It's ok, you signed a prenup". I said, "Oh really? Show it to me!" and he asked for five business days. I was completely shocked and scared at what was about to be unleashed on me falsely. And the next two years of legal war began.

I went to my son's school the next morning to drop him off. Something inside me told me to check in with the staff to find out who was the emergency contact for my son and who was authorized to pick him up from school. He had the "other woman" authorized to pick up my son! Always check these things because when something doesn't feel right it probably isn't. I cannot get into details of what happened in court. I will say, however, that the "other woman" and he were continuing to lie to her husband and whoever else he was dating. But, it was ugly. I was constantly fearful for my life—my school, teachers, friends, clients who would come to me for hair letting me practice and learn my craft, and my family who called me every day. The other woman testified against me. It was nuts! She got caught lying under oath so many times until finally his lawyer told her to stop talking.

Insert a letter to the "other woman":

Dear former best friend,

I heard you were not OK. I found out what you "attempted" to do to yourself. Please know he is not worth that. Please know that I cried for you when I found out. Also, no, I don't want to hurt you for what you did. I actually pray for you almost every day. I'm not upset with you and I forgave you already a long time ago. You need to see past money. You were so beautiful already to me before you lost all that weight. I still giggle when I think about you calling people names who hurt me, (nitwit/osti lol). I appreciate all the times you made me mentally prepared to leave him when you were my shoulder to cry on. Please stop fighting with your ex-husband. You are showing your daughter the worst example and I don't want her to repeat your mistakes. She will remember all of this. It isn't too late for you to change and do the right things from now on. I will continue to be praying for you. Our song will always be Sia, "Elastic Heart". When I listen to it, I realize I do have one. I can be pulled down to the depths of pain and yet bounce right back up, and it sounds to me like you cannot.

We did everything together. I believed you when I cried to you, and you told me I deserved better. I think your husband deserved better, too. You and my ex are actually a lot alike, so it makes sense why y'all were attracted to each other when the darkness set in.

Best wishes to you and your family, your daughter was like a niece to me and I did love her. I would have done anything to help your family and I appreciate how you treated my son. I do believe you probably somewhere in there feel guilty because I was probably the best friend you ever had and I want to give you my blessing to let it go. I am grateful.

God Bless Your Heart,

Tiff (sending you emotional flowers)

He spent four hundred and fifty thousand dollars on both of our attorneys' fees fighting his own lies to divorce me. My husband's immediate family wanted me gone. His lies and threats and complete torture were nothing I could ever even be mentally prepared for. Through forensics and catching his lies we proved that the prenup was forged. He actually did make it in Florida three days before our wedding and faxed it to some lawyer from our honeymoon in Maui from the Ritz Carlton, behind my back. This is where I want to shift from my Hell to help you. Things that were said to me. Things I learned. Things that helped me at the worst moment in my life.

Of course, I had to withdraw from running for Mrs. Illinois because I was no longer going to be a Mrs. The director cried with me as I told her what happened and she told me she was praying for me. I found a place that was my secret escape. I found a horse farm that was open to the public every day during long hours. I started visiting the beautiful stallions and mustangs. I went there a lot. I went to cry and talk to them and they would collect my tears and let me kiss them and they listened and sometimes made me smile. They slowly reminded me of that little girl in Georgia. The one who would ride freely and so gracefully and beautifully jump over any obstacles that came her way. The girl who wasn't afraid. The girl who was happy.

If you are in a situation like mine, or just wanting to file for divorce and you are scared, it is completely normal. I know men and women who just want to leave and feel like the "bad guy" for wanting more for themselves and just to be mentally healthy. Divorce is just so common, yet so complicated and the most important and serious thing you may ever do that affects your entire life and if you have children, theirs too. Taking the step to call a lawyer and being afraid of how to pay for it whether you are the financially supportive spouse or not is so absolutely terrifying. Everyone kept telling me not to listen to all the things my soon-to-be-ex (STBX) was saying to me. Looking back, he was saying so many things that weren't even true or going to happen. He was trying to scare me, negotiate with me, threaten me and destroy me. What he said when his mouth was moving actually meant zero, zilch, nothing! I wasted so much time and energy worrying about it.

Living with a soon-to-be cheating lying terrifying ex is a nightmare that nobody should ever experience. Lawyers and court and fear and everything being taken from me, I had come to a point when I was sleeping at a friend's house hiding with my child, crying as she read me Bible scriptures (angel). No matter what, I kept going to school every day. He told me every time he could that I was a "beauty school dropout", which only kept me working harder to finish. Fortunately, the judge gave me the money to stay in a cheap hotel during his parenting time since I had no family around and nowhere to go. He had to stay away from the house when I had my parenting time. They called it "nesting". I was scared every day that my food would be poisoned or someone would break in and murder me. I would get into that hotel room and journal and drink and cry and I felt safe like I was hiding, but I missed my son in ways I could not describe.

You cannot record anyone without permission. You cannot hack their devices or there are huge consequences. Texts mean nothing in court. Of course, they will try to accuse you of being a drinker or whatever else. Of course, you will ask yourself how this person who supposedly loved you could be so evil. Divorce is absolute hell. If there is one ounce left inside you that there can possibly be any chance to save or salvage the relationship, fight like you have never fought to stay together. If there is not, get help. Even if you have to call one hundred attorneys or shelters or advocacy centers please do not take any steps on your own.

I had a three day garage sale that my sweet friend from beauty school helped me with. Selling all the baby items and items that reminded me of our twenty year relationship was heartbreaking. I had kept every bib and pacifier and blanket. I wanted more children and I wanted a big family. I could not have done it without her (angel). That sweet young beauty school friend of mine held me as I sobbed selling each and every item and tried to laugh with me as we played with all the toys and said goodbye to them for another child to enjoy. The judge ordered us to sell our home to prevent things from dragging on in court.

It sold in three days to the first people who looked at it and they offered a fifteen day close, even after he flooded the basement and I had to call a friend's husband (angel) to come clean it up the day before it got shown. I had one weekend in my mind to get the money I needed from the judge to get an apartment. I got it. When we moved from that giant unhappy home URGENTLY I took just what I needed.

There was a garage in the apartment and I was able to use it as storage and I didn't mind parking outside. While at that little apartment, my son and I literally danced all night and day every day. It was gated and safe and there was a pool and a grill and a free cappuccino machine and a gym. If a light bulb went out, I just made a phone call and someone would fix it. I taught myself how to grill like a boss that summer! I know I am very fortunate to have had that. I was grateful every single day even to just be alone. It only broke my heart when he had to take my son from me every week for a couple of nights. Those were the hardest times to cope with in my entire life.

Letting go of material things was not hard for me anymore. I think I was starting to see in my new apartment that I had just what I needed, not stuff that I wanted. I kind of think in some ways God was taking a little more of the spoiled brat out of me. I didn't care about brand names anymore. I sold my designer handbags to a girl from my beauty school who cried tears of joy that she would never be able to afford before. I was happy just to have meat in the freezer for my son and I to eat. I was happy for the coffee I was drinking. I was happy to have warm water to shower in. I was grateful for the elderly neighbor woman who walked her dog past me every morning and gave me advice as I sipped my coffee on my balcony (angel). I had so many amazing single friends I was meeting! I was dating and super healthy and skinny and starting to feel like the most beautiful I have ever looked!

I started swimming. A lot. I was swimming and swimming almost every day, about sixty laps a day. I meditated in that pool. I could cry, scream, laugh, pray, and talk to myself in complete silence and with no distractions under the water. Ironically, my dear friend who was the therapist who I would go on walks with when I was married before and encouraged me to go back to school... well, she was dropped on her tail by her husband and started going through a divorce too. She moved into the apartment across from me and I had her by my side and she had me. We even shared the same lawyer and it was a gift from God that my sweet friend and I had each other.

My son's favorite thing about that time at the apartment, he always says, was our "midnight swims". Randomly, I would put him to bed and be up talking on the phone or texting as I usually do. In the middle of the night I would put on a bikini and sneak in to wake him up with his swim trunks in my hands. You have never seen a child jump up and change that fast ever! We would just swim under the stars and play and celebrate our beautiful new freedom. He had summer camp during the week and I was still in beauty school trying to be happy.

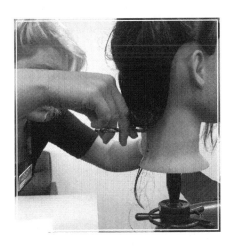

My friends all still came to me at the beauty school for hair and makeup and waxing. I quickly became number one at my school. I set records they had never seen. My teachers were my friends. My peers were my sounding board as I told them the ugly side of divorce hoping they will never have to go through this. I began having up to thirteen clients a day, part time, in four hours. I had a three-month waiting list eventually. The clients I saw each day were angels, too, sent to me from God to give me whatever lesson or advice I needed specifically at that time.

Whether it was someone to pray over me, laugh with me, listen and hug me and let me sob, teach me about home buying, counsel me, remind me of skills I forgot on how to own a car or home, and even see the signs when he was trying to take a home equity loan out in my name, my clients each day were in my chair for a reason! And at the same time, I was getting very good at making them look absolutely beautiful. I started to be ok when my son went to his dad's. (Of course his dad bought him a home in the most upscale town next to mine). I started to be OK choosing to be alone and not even drinking when my son was gone. I started being OK not going on dates trying to find a man to cling to. I started to lean back and see the angels God was sending me all day every day if I just opened my eyes and looked.

Two years of absolute hell had gone by, and then, I graduated from cosmetology school at thirty-nine years old. The divorce finally ended. I took a settlement for half of what I was fighting for, but it was OK and I would be OK. I bought a home back in my old neighborhood in order to keep my son's school and friends and teachers the same, as he wished. I built a beautiful salon in it. Blushing Inc. was a legit licensed and insured salon! I had about seventy-five clients at graduation and my teachers were so proud of me. I could not have done it without them, my friends, my clients, and my son and his calm and patient way of motivating me, but being proud of me. I passed the state cosmetology exam and I was ready to work!

What does freedom mean to you? Do you have it? Are you working in the career that you are happy doing? Is there something more you would like to do? It isn't too late! Even if you are madly in love with the greatest man on the planet, freedom can be your best friend.

MR. MRS. **MS.** MISS. ME.

PART 3:

"MS."

Whatever the title is, queen, love
yourself.

MS. AS A POWERFUL QUEEN

This is how the second half starts. At forty years old, I sit here a Ms. This is not the end, however, because I feel like this is the beginning. I am brand new again, like I am starting over. I have been divorced for two years. My son is nine years old. I have a lot going on and a lot to tell you if you are reading this. You are reading this because maybe you are a Ms. now, too. You are divorced or about to be. You are scared. Maybe you have no money. Maybe you have no job. Maybe you are the breadwinner and have to support an ex. Maybe you are just so confused. I have survived complete and utter trauma. This is the part of the story of how I got through it and rose up to becoming a beauty queen, despite being thrown in the trash by a man I loved.

(Christmas card photo shoot, 1-year post-divorce)

TELLING YOUR CHILD(REN)

When you go through divorce and children are involved, in the state of Illinois you are both required to go to "parental counseling". My counselor was absolutely amazing. I was so pleased when I met her that she let me cry and held my hand and gave me Godly amazing advice. The best part was how she helped me tell my son. She said, "Grab three green crayons and three brown crayons and a piece of paper. Draw in the one brown crayon a tree trunk. Write your son's name in it. Then draw a branch going off his trunk with his color of green leaves. In each leaf write the name of his teachers, coaches, friends. Then, in your brown crayon draw your branch. Draw your green leaves with the names of your family, friends, mentors, etc." And reluctantly, my ex drew his branch and his family and his leaves, rolling his eyes at how absolutely annoying I was being. I was explaining to my son that he is always going to be the trunk of our family tree. How in life, we will add new leaves as they grow on our branches and some leaves will fall off. However, Mommy and Daddy's branches are "growing apart", but you will always be the trunk of our tree. She said it's better than using words such as split or separate for him to understand.

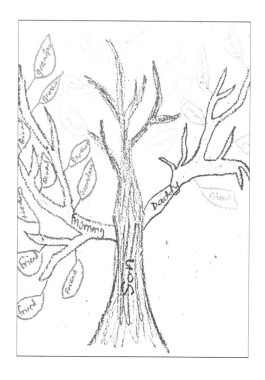

It worked beautifully. I was absolutely relieved he wasn't sad or scared one bit, he said. I also had gone to church and somehow, in my chair sobbing, a man approached me with a team of seven pastors and stood around me and prayed over me. I did it. Maybe somehow it really was putting the nail in the coffin. I knew after telling my son, I would never look back.

I have met so many people in the past three years that are divorcing and men or women that put their children in the middle of way too much pain. It is unacceptable and so sad to me. Children and teenagers are not capable of processing divorce. Heck, I wasn't even able to process it at times as an adult. If you cannot see past your personal agenda to protect your children from being uncomfortable, scared and confused, please seek help. There are so many resources you can find for help and it is your responsibility as a parent to do so. Never be afraid to call upon counselors, police, or DCFS to investigate if something doesn't feel right. The responsibility is greater than the fear and the people who are there to help will guide you and support you, even if you are just taking precautions. If you don't, you could be just as guilty in allowing bad behavior to happen to your child(ren).

I cannot encourage you enough to use a co-parenting app in order to communicate with an ex who is controlling or narcissistic or verbally abusive or scaring you. Text messages are not always applicable in court because they can be made.

The best coping mechanism I ever advise people of when dealing with a narcissist is the "grey rock method" developed by Ellen Biros, MS, SCSW, a therapist in Georgia. You cannot change someone's behavior. They have to change it themselves. What you can do is be completely like a grey rock and give them absolutely nothing. They will, hopefully, eventually get bored and find another victim to feed their need to put others down to feed themselves. Once you have mastered this, you will feel more at peace and away from the drama and attacks.

And remember, if you question if you are a crazy person or a narcissistic person, congratulations you aren't one. Someone who is a narc would never even ask themselves that question. We hear about children or teenagers who get bullied, but sometimes as an adult you can be too. They want to make you afraid. Use your resources and stand up for yourself. Writing this book even has me afraid. So, I am doing this to speak up and speak the truth and taking that risk to show myself I am not afraid and to let you know you are not alone.

Co-parenting is an ongoing struggle. Most break ups allow you to block and delete. When you have a responsibility to a child or children to put your personal needs or wants aside for the better wishes for them, you are a hero. Even when you find yourself alone and your ex has a new partner and begins taking responsibility and time for your child. I cried for three days when I found out my son met my ex's new girlfriend. I wanted so badly to hate her. I called my mom hysterically crying. She said to me, "Honey, you are thirty-nine years old and who are you calling right now?" Instantly, I stopped crying and realized I will always be my son's mama. The thoughts and feelings of being replaced were silly and not true. Now, I see her as the glorified nanny. I hope and imagine, at least my ex will be on better behavior when he's with her. And just maybe, one day he will have another person who loves him, too.

I know there were times that I felt like it wasn't fair. How can he and his new girlfriend play "house" and have holidays and be happy with my son and I am alone? I have no family around for my holidays when it is his turn to take my son. Sure, my friends and their families invite me over, but I don't want to be that girl that cries in the corner on their special day with their family. So, I am learning how to have holidays alone and not cry and just be thankful that I don't have to spend it with nasty family members who made me feel like crap just because I existed and didn't have on the perfect shoes.

It is my mission and goal because of having the world's best step-dad, that is my dad, to find that kind of love and support for my son one day. However, being that my biological father left us at such a young age and refuses to even recognize my sister and I as his children, I would never want that to happen to my son. Even if I cannot be around or communicate with his dad without using an app or wanting to have him in my life, I would never stop his father from being in his. I put myself on the back burner in order to have my son have two parents. My ex does want to be in my son's life and I would never want that to stop for my selfish reasons.

He bad-mouths me to my child. He criticizes me for not having a four year degree. He tries to control and spy and manipulate me still. I always say, "You have to love to hate." I don't hate him. I just don't care. Maybe, in time, the threats, and the verbal abuse, and the false accusations that I defend, and the "hate" will stop. In the meantime, all I can do is pray and co-parent with God and stay truly happy for myself and my son. Faith is what you have when faith is all you have. The more you appreciate the blessings and trust God, the more blessings and peace you have. I learned to love myself enough to not base any fears on my past trauma. Every day is new and every experience is new. I can always rest my head on my pillow at night and trust and believe that I am doing the right things.

MS. INDEPENDENT AGAIN

I finally did it. The day the divorce ended and I became a Ms. I felt so relieved. My attorney hugged me goodbye and said the nicest things like in a fatherly way. I wanted to do one of those jumps with my hands in the air and my feet clicking together in the air sideways! I was meeting my amazing realtor friend and looking at houses to buy in my old neighborhood. I wanted my son's wish to keep his same friends and teachers to come true. I found my home. I did it and I was ready to move! I realize, by the way, that this isn't always the case. I am so unbelievably appreciative that I had the ability to buy a new home just in time for school to start back in the same old neighborhood. I know my son loved it there and even though driving past the old memories bothered me for a little while, we made new ones. I have new wonderful and respectful neighbors. We have healthy friendships. I am the queen of my own beautiful castle.

Moving day...the movers started around 3:00 in the afternoon. I was alone, but I worked hard and so did they. Around 9:00 p.m. I heard yelling and screaming coming from the driveway. They were fighting and punching each other! I called the manager hiding in my backyard to just get them to finish and come back the next day for the second load. When they finally left my neighbor came over with wine. She said they were pulled over down the street with eight cop cars getting arrested! She said, "You checked your valuables right?" and I got that sick stomach pain in my whole body. I ran upstairs only to notice...my wedding ring was gone. Fast forward a year after losing that battle with the moving company I received a call from the president of the moving company. He offered me a settlement (more than I would've gotten pawning it) and after hearing my story gave an additional $5,000 to my charity of choice! God waited until a pandemic and for me to have the perfect people to give that money to. I didn't want to keep the ring, anyways, but how amazing that it turned into help for children in need!

Being in my new home was off to a rocky start and I was incredibly overwhelmed. I didn't know anything about managing a home. He did everything to paying the bills and hiring everyone who managed what he couldn't do. The financial part I began to handle, but I didn't even own a drill. I have the most amazing neighbors who have helped me when my garage door broke and when the world's most humongous spider was on my wall! I keep it so clean because it is my precious home. I graduated and built a salon in the front room. I cry tears of joy when I wake up almost every morning. Did you know you have to change the filters in your AC unit every three months? And if you travel it is important to turn the water off so the pipes don't burst while you're gone and flood? And yardwork is much more work than you think and takes constant attention. Now I know why my dad made me do so much back then. When I look at what I am doing as a single woman alone, I am grateful. I even completed thirty-seven bags of mulch all by myself!

There are a lot of people that give me quotes for handyman services or work and they almost always say, "Go talk to your husband and let me know". I say, "Umm.. no I don't have one" and instantly the price quote sent to me is a joke. I have to work harder to keep getting quotes about double or triple the amounts until I find someone who can give me what the work is actually worth.

Maintaining a home alone is not as scary as I thought it would be. I am also more sympathetic to the amount of responsibility that falls on a man's shoulders and the pressure they feel to be the rock of the home. A lot of men I have dated actually seem intimidated by my home and my independence. I think sometimes I don't give myself enough credit for how far I have come. My ex and his family have fancy cars and mansions. I just want this peaceful, clean, happy, safe home of mine.

As I muse on what it means to be a Ms., I wonder if there can be a bit of it in all of us women. Men get to keep the title of Mr. no matter what in life (of course, unless they become a doctor, or reverend or something, but women can do that too!). But, aren't all women Ms. no matter what? To me, it just means we are leaning into the woman that we always have been growing into. Confidence, intelligence, independence, kind and nurturing, no matter what or who is connecting to us. We have strength to be whoever we choose to be and loving and supporting ourselves and not listening to anyone who says we can't do something. We can rise above what happens TO us and be defined by what we do anyways.

MS. AS A SINGLE GIRL

Let us switch gears again and discuss the freedom that comes with being able to date and answer to only yourself for the first time in a long time. When I first filed for divorce, I started implementing mommy time and daddy time. I had to start that practice for my son. Living in the same home as my ex for two years during divorce was absolutely horrific. However, I want to talk about the steps I took, healthy or not, because everyone I know that has gone through or goes through this has a coping mechanism. Mine became a school which was a positive, but I went through quite a ride dating again. I am going to use fake names for this next part. However, the dating stories are real and some were better than others. The people I am about to highlight each taught me things over the course of three years. There were other "dates" that all were learning lessons, but these are the most important or, even, the most eye opening and entertaining. It's a funny thing when a guy asks me if he is in the book...I just smile and say "What would your nickname be?" and "You have to buy the book to find out!" Hahahaha!

First date ever...I was with a girlfriend and we did vision boards and joined a dating app on New Year's Eve in the heart of my divorce. The vision board had pictures of sexy men and vacation and business goals and bikinis. I had a goal there to open a salon and even publish a book! I wanted so badly for my divorce to be over. I wanted independence, confidence, success financially, love, and happiness. I was excited, but also terrified. I posted my best pictures on Bumble and began swiping. (Which, looking back, I was nowhere even ready to be in another relationship until, for me, was well over a year post divorce being finalized.)

"Hero":

I met "Hero". Meeting him at that restaurant I remembered feeling like I was being watched or spied on and I told him. "This is your first date ever after filing for divorce?" he said. I replied, "Yes, and I am so scared." He looked at me with those big green eyes looking like a combination of The Rock and Vin Diesel and said, "See that man at the bar behind me reading the newspaper?" I gasped and looked around and I said "Yes, why?" He lifted his shirt up to show me his badge and gun and said, "Just kidding. I'm not scared." This wonderful man. He was kind and gentle and respectful. We facetimed a lot and only got to be together briefly as he was a hero and traveled all over the country fighting terrorists. Supposedly. I am still friends with him today years later and I still don't know quite how to feel about him. It wasn't that serious, and I haven't seen him since, but I am extremely grateful to have met him and I hope he is watching over me like he says he is. He is a hero to me because he is strong and respectful and made me feel like we were dancing when we were together. He also could sense it sometimes when I would need help or when I would be in my bathroom crying and would call me to say, "Chin up, beautiful". Thank you, Hero, wherever you are. You were sweet and kind and a gentleman. You are a bit of a mystery to me, but I am glad for our friendship and the time you helped me and listened.

"High School Crush":

He saw my post on Instagram with the caption, "He always hated these jeans", with my ass looking fire! He got in my DM's and who knew that sexy man was ten years divorced! And he still thinks I was the one that got away? Well, I got in my car and drove straight to my hometown to his house. We danced and laughed and he was even sexier as a man than as a teenager. Our connection to music and art and his calm, loving, artistic, sensitive demeanor was breathtaking. I was definitely not in a place to date. But, living in the house with the person who wanted me to die the most in the whole world, my crush would stay up late and talk to me and let me cry. He has a son and would refuse to leave his side, which is an absolutely beautiful thing. I still talk to him almost daily. I love you High School Crush. You are one of my best friends and I still dream of one day us taking that vacation together, however, I worry we will never want to leave. We have watched each other get our hearts broken. When you are sad, I'm sad. I still come across certain songs and dream about you. Cheers to when we can listen together and dance again with my lips on your neck. Thank you for being one of my best friends.

"The Catfish":

I don't even remember his name, but this was a

significant story. Picture this, my soon to be ex parading around the house yawning and stretching like he just got his +_(*&^ sucked every morning as I made my coffee with my head down wanting to run away, but pushing it down because my son was watching. I got on the dating app again (I take breaks often when it makes me feel overwhelmed, disappointed, anxious, or afraid). I met a nice guy who said he was a high school youth soccer coach and a businessman in downtown Chicago. He asked me to dinner. This was the first time in my life I have ever taken an Uber alone anywhere. I was so nervous and my STBX waved out the front door and I could barely look at him as he said, "If you need me just call". WTF!? So, off I went.

I got to the bar/restaurant and got a drink. I was so scared and uncomfortable. Ten minutes later he was supposed to arrive. Fifteen, twenty minutes later, it was like panic set in. I called the date and he hit the end button on the first ring! I was starving, realizing I hadn't eaten in about a week. I must've looked like a deer in headlights (black velvet dress and black tights with black heels). A super sweet couple (angels) at the bar said, "Are you OK dear?" and that was all it took. I started sobbing. They asked me to sit by them and eat. I did and they just listened. As I ordered my Uber to go home and climbed in, I realized it was only 8:30 p.m.! I was embarrassed and didn't want to look like a total loser coming home so early to my mean ex who would laugh at me.

I was hyperventilating and snot dripping all over my jacket in the back seat of my Uber. After about five minutes of it, the driver said, "Where are we getting a drink?" I replied, "I'm not paying an Uber driver to hang out with me!" then I told him what had happened. He pulled into a little local bar by my house and said, "Get out". We had drinks and laughed and talked all night. He looked at his watch and said, "It's midnight. Let's take you home." And home I went thanking him for being such a great friend that night. I didn't cry again that night. He showed me so much humanity and kindness that I needed so badly at that moment. Thank you sweet Uber driver for being my sidekick that night so I didn't look like a fool, and you turned my tears into a smile and laughter so I didn't look like a loser.

Rebound Man aka "Baby":

I was approached by a super-hot guy one night outside of a bar with my girlfriends. He later found me on Facebook and started chatting with me. He was incredible. He was also much younger than me, but so much fun. I was in a completely broken state. So was he. We did so much together that whole summer and I thought I loved him. One day, I asked him to go to church with me and he broke up with me. I was crushed. I cried more over him than my ex-husband-to be. I remember watching "Star is

Born" with Lady Gaga and Bradley Cooper and I realized he was an alcoholic. It was a sickness that I had never seen and there was nothing I could do about it. He tried many times to come back and would quit drinking, then start again and be out of control. Living with his parents at twenty-eight years old, there was no hope for us. The memories we shared were so fun and went so fast as if it was a dream. I'm actually grateful for the time we shared and that I got that rebound out of my system and survived. It was wild! I still think of him often and hope he is okay. He taught me to feel beautiful and young again and called me his Barbie doll. I just had to move on and he knew I was not going to rescue him.

"The Coach":

This guy isn't so much a dating person, but more of a guy best friend. He could be the funniest, sweetest and dirtiest man in the world. He's also married to one of my best friends and gives me advice and support even when I do extremely stupid things. He is worth mentioning because he has taught me that "every guy that tries to talk to you wants to sleep with you. Learn it and get over it." I mean who knew that men were so visual and simple? I think they need to have periods so they are forced to take a week off each month so they can see straight! I love him and his wife for allowing us to be friends and I know how much they love each other unconditionally and it is actually inspiring. Thank you, Coachy Coach for always being my cheerleader and guiding me through the man's mind, but never judging me for making mistakes and wanting me to just be safe. You will always be the man who makes me laugh the most. I love you.

"Dr. Jordan":

I met a guy online who said he was a physical therapist. We had three incredible dates and got along very well. For some reason I was trying to Google him, as I usually do, and I couldn't find him. I asked him what his last name was again and he said he needed to talk to me in person. He came to talk to me and let me know his "real" name. I guessed it right away, "You're married, aren't you?" He said, "Yes". I kicked him out and after Googling, I saw he was a doctor and his wife was all over his website for his practices talking about what a great doctor he was. Turns out he wasn't even using his own photos. Somehow he found pictures of some guy that looks just like him for the app! Watch out girls, he's still on there. I am not going to be the reason his wife gets absolutely destroyed the way I was. I just learned so much from that. If you cannot Google them and get all the information prior to the first date, don't go.

"The Best Friend":

Every time I have thought of having another female to trust as my best friend it terrifies me. Until I met her. She is the most beautiful female I have ever laid eyes on in the flesh. I didn't realize until two years into our friendship that I, unconsciously, created a "bestie test" for any guys I had interest in. And even though her gut is 100% instinctually on point, she knows within one second of laying eyes on a guy that he is wrong for me, before I can even put her in front of them to see if they will like her better than me. I have apologized for it, I realized I was doing it and it's not fair to her. This amazing woman just loves me and wants the best for me. I also want the best for her. What she shows me more than anything is how to be smart, guarded, picky, patient, kind, loving, a fighter, and a bad ass chick at all times. I admire her strength and beauty and I could never find another woman like her.

She has my back like a sister and she wipes my tears and builds me up like a sister. Sometimes, I think back to when I cried and prayed for a single friend when I was going through my divorce because everyone I knew was married. God answered my prayers by sending me her. I would do anything for her and love her for the rest of my life. She has taught me so much and behind me will forever be this beautiful powerhouse of a woman showing me to have no fear and chase my dreams, but keep my chin up high and never settle for less than what I deserve. I love you, bestie. You taught me how to trust the most beautiful female best friend again. This is what she taught me:

> Girls are like
> apples on trees. The best
> ones are at the top of the tree.
> The boys don't want to reach for
> the good ones because they are afraid
> of falling and getting hurt. Instead, they
> just get the rotten apples from the ground
> that aren't as good, but easy. So the apples
> at the top think something is wrong with
> them, when in reality, they're amazing.
> They just have to wait for the right
> boy to come along, the one
> who's brave enough
> to climb
> all the way
> to the top
> of the tree.

"The Mooch":

Let's start by saying,

Rule #1, never ever ever be with someone who is not fully divorced and healed (at least one year for me). This man manipulated me into "playing house" in my own house and was deceiving me the entire time as a tool to make his soon to be ex-wife jealous. I had just bought my own home and thought I was ready to love someone and let them in. Subconsciously, I thought I needed a man and couldn't do it by myself. I let him be around my son and his kids were in my home often. I was so blissfully happy to have a partner again that I didn't see what was happening.

Rule #2, I will never ever ever let anyone play house with my son until at least six months to a year of dating. I beat myself up for so long for allowing my son see me get hurt again. I found out he was cheating and lying to me. Someone told me that it was okay that I made that mistake once, but not to ever do that again. Steve Harvey's book, "Think Like a Lady, Act Like a Man" says that it is normal to want to show a man you're dating your child(ren) because they make up so much of who you are and they need to see the entire picture. So, I understand why I did it, but begging my son to forgive me for letting him wipe my tears AGAIN and finding out he was not my priority for that time because I was weak and careless brought me more guilt than anything I have ever felt in my entire life. I made my son a promise. I told him "the only man that will ever break Mommy's heart again is you..so don't break it!" and he laughed and kissed me and said he would never and I know that.

My dear friend who is a Harvard Law graduate also slapped the attention in my face that there is something called "Squatters Rights" or "Adverse Possession". I have found that it is different in every state, however someone who is occupying your home and paying towards the property has rights and can cause you extreme legal problems if they don't want to leave. Also, if you are acting as a spouse with someone, (cohabitating), you need to make sure you talk to your lawyer because in some cases if you receive alimony or child support the payer can make it less or even stop it in court if someone is "acting" as your husband. So, needless to say, nobody will be squatting in or mooching off my home or life ever again until it is someone I know I will want to be with the rest of my life. How do they even get a right to "act" as a step-father to my child? He has a father who earned that right. I even have one client in the salon who's second husband purchased her home from her just to make sure she knew he was taking the steps to be her provider and keep her children in the same home. Wow!

Rule #3, the honeymoon phase/infatuation stage is real. Most say three to four months and true colors show. I think of it like a new job. Steve Harvey also references this in his book as the "probationary period". As in, "they don't get the benefits until they have proven themselves in the first ninety days". He is more referring to sex, however, I also think it counts for more and I will never ever make that mistake again.

Speaking of sex, get an STD test every six months/ one year if you are sexually active. I made mistakes. At one point in a relationship I got an IUD. There are so many men out there and women who use the apps to hook up. I am fortunate to have my amazing gynecologist. He listened while I cried to him and told him to take it out. It was the ultimate enabler. I needed to vow to myself that any man

I sleep with uses a condom. I also find that not sleeping with men even after six dates, I end up dropping them or they fade away. I made mistakes. My gynecologist would allow me to tell him anything and he wanted to help me stay safe and also understood what I was going through. He delivered my son. He knows me. I was confused and stupid and he allowed me to tell him that I was careless. I care so much about my body and that includes my woman parts. They are perfect and I cannot allow anyone to take that away from me. I am a mother and I need to be healthy in order for the right man to cherish me.

"The Mooch" cheated on me with the woman he was divorcing (his wife). I didn't know until about six months later. I will never let that happen again. He love-bombed me, he lied to me, and he made me cry to my son again and I can never let a man make me cry to my son ever again. However, the guy his soon-to-be-ex-wife was seeing is now one of my best friends. We connected months after the break ups and compared notes and laughed and talked for over three hours. We hang out sometimes now and he never makes me feel pressured or weird. We are there for each other and we can talk about anything. He is one of the most important people to me and if it weren't for that moochy jerk, we never would have met. For that, I am forever grateful.

"Mr. Sinny Sin":

I met a man online. He clearly stated "God First". We chatted and eventually talked on the phone and I was looking forward to meeting him. He was so so so so so so so so hot, like Gaston from Beauty and the Beast! He had an hour of free time one evening that I was free to meet at a restaurant near the place he had to take his son for Bible study. Awwwww! That day I was beaming with excitement as I had just been selected to represent Illinois in the Ms. World International Pageant! When we met I was so blown away with joy and he was incredible. We laughed and talked on the patio outside alone and he walked me to my car and kissed me so passionately I felt like I couldn't even see. Driving home every song was telling me my life was changed and two miracles happened in the same day! He and I texted that night about how absolutely amazing we thought each other was. Then, he invited me to come over, literally the night we met for an hour. I said 'no'. His son was there and I am not interested in that awkwardness for a child and I only met him one time for an hour. I ended up having some of my friends stop by my home because of my amazing pageant news and I told him I look forward to seeing him again, but not comfortable going to his home. The next morning I hoped so badly to receive a "good morning beautiful"' text and by 11:00 a.m. when I heard nothing I texted. "Good morning?" I said. He said nothing. By 1:00 p.m. I was so disappointed to see he deleted me from the app and I texted one more time. "Are you ghosting me? What did I do wrong?" and again, nothing. Still to this day nothing. I don't understand why someone who is a Christian would not respect a woman that just isn't looking for a hook-up. Do people really use God as an excuse? Maybe he had a girlfriend and just had one free night? Why is someone ghosting me making me completely question myself? Ghosting is a coward move. I guess I will never know, but God said, "Nope!" too! Did he know he was a liar and just wanted to hook up and knew I was better than that and he wanted to protect me? Either way, thanks Mr. Sinny Sin. Rejection is God's protection! God Bless youuuuuuuuuuuu!

"Hot Mess":

I talked to him for a month all day every day before even meeting him. We were in the beginning of a pandemic and everyone was quarantining and I even got Covid-19. He was brought into my life at a time I was alone and scared and eventually in the hospital. It was incredible how when he and I met he was driving through my home town in Georgia on a family trip to Florida with his kids and even stopped at my home peach orchard to send me pictures and let me know that he was there for me, especially when I was alone and scared. This was the first time I thought I knew so much about someone before even meeting him. We talked and facetimed for a month before even meeting. The first date was so lovely. We were so nervous and excited and he blew me away. He was a lot like me in our mindfulness and creativity and passion for life. He was plenty healed post his divorce and seemed like a wonderful father. I kept feeling so much anxiety about him for some reason, though, and I hated the way his social media made me worry and question everything. However, he made me feel for the first time in my life like I was being carried and my feet never touched the ground. He made me feel like the most beautiful doll in the world. Until he hit the end of the honeymoon phase and maybe just thought to himself "what am I doing?" Which I have heard is a thing for men. Sometimes, he would send me sexy pictures of himself working out and then I would see him posting them on his Facebook and Instagram. It made me think he was trying to get attention like I was when I had to post on my pageant pages. I even told him, "I thought those pictures were for me?" and it was embarrassing to anyone who knew I was dating him when they looked him up and he looked like an idiot. The push pull effect he gave me as I stayed loyal and consistent to his needs got to be too much and I ended it. Only to then receive a DM on Facebook from a former girlfriend of his a week after the breakup that he was trying to be with her the entire time he was seeing me. He made me realize that he was creepy and that I only saw him through my loving eyes. Once I didn't anymore, I saw him back on the dating app and my stomach instantly did a flip and I am proud of myself for not feeling pain from a break up for the first time. I realized I did love him, but he doesn't deserve me. At forty-six years old, he is a hot mess and just not my equal. I am, however, grateful for meeting his amazing sister, who is a queen, herself.

"Mr. Danger":

I had a guy I was talking to for months. One night I finally let him come by and "hang out". I was very clear with him that we would not be hooking up. He went to my gym and I felt comfortable that we were friends. He had a horrible day and his car had died and he was hungry. I let him come over so I could be a listening ear and feed him, as he seemed like he needed a friend. We were chatting and having a few drinks. He tried to kiss me and touch me and I said 'no'. He got very angry and he was not taking "No" for an answer. He slammed my back and butt against the kitchen drawer handle so hard that it sent a jolt of pain throughout my whole back. As I curled up in pain and shock saying "OUCH!" he grabbed my wrist and slammed my arm against another drawer and I went nuts! I fought him. I screamed and grabbed my phone to call 9-1-1. He finally left and the tears I cried for so long after that I swore to never let anyone come over to my home again. I am so lucky to have not been raped or had damage done to my body permanently. It made me feel so absolutely awful that I only told my two best friends the details. I felt like I was the one in the wrong and it definitely wasn't the case. It is people like that that make me build the walls of my castle up even higher. I feel like a true queen alone in the safety of my home and I will not be able to trust again for a little while. Please be safe and listen to me when I say don't learn the hard way. Protect your home and your safety. I never want anyone to have anything like this happen to you, and this is why I am sharing this story with you.

"Mr. Don't Settle'

I met a guy once who had most of the list checked off. I could see past some of his flaws because he really did want to "work with me". He was attractive, we had great chemistry, he followed all the "rules." He was consistent. He had less than average goals. Yet, as time went on I couldn't help but think he wasn't at my level. He didn't make me laugh the way my son does. He always had a critique. Even when it was about random things that happened to him all day long. Altogether, he was a decent person and a good single dad to his children. He would've done anything for me, except he did not believe in God. I gave it a fighting chance, hoping for a sign. After four months on and off, out of nowhere, I got a dick pic instead. And when I did not "praise his pee pee", I was out. He's blocked.

I have always known it to be OK to go on dates and say, "No thank you". Some of my closest friends now are men. Maybe they want to stay friends with me just to be kind and helpful and care about being a part of my life anyways. Then, there are others who cannot handle even being friends with me if I do not feel a romantic connection with them. It hurts me when I want a friendship with a man and he feels hurt when I don't love him. The part of dating I dislike the most is rejecting someone and also when I get feelings for someone and I have that stomach churning feeling in my gut that something isn't right. The only other thing left is true love. So, if you're single and afraid to date, I completely understand why. I guess it takes a lot of courage and strength to date because of the millions of single men out there, there's only one "the one" in the next part of our lives, we hope to find. A lot of people I see find love the second time around quicker and easier than me. I don't feel like "how can they find love and I can't?" anymore. I think I am supposed to keep going on my journey to the top first, so that when I do find someone, he is my equal. My ex-husband drilled into my head for twenty years "If you ever leave me, good luck. The best you will ever get is a grocery store bagger or gas station attendant". I used to think, well then, I will find the sexiest most incredible gas station man in the world! (Not that there's anything wrong with those men!) I just want someone who is able to handle my goals and my ambition properly. He cannot be intimidated by it or try to compete or belittle me. He also cannot suffocate me from staying focused on my dreams. Men need to have goals, work ethic, make me feel safe and beautiful, give back to their community, and be confident in themselves. Also, they need to respect a woman and build a friendship first, every time. I just want them to be fun and make me laugh...not at their junk in the pants.

There is a lot to learn about men and dating. Dating apps and going on dates and rules and navigating the ghosting and love-bombing and catfishing and married cheaters and fakes are everywhere! Facebook dating is nice because you can see who you are mutual friends with that is also single. However, there are a lot of fakes on there and it consumes a lot of your time. Bumble is fun and there are a lot of really hot guys that use it. The woman makes the first move, but often the second move a guy makes is sending a picture of his junk and you have to be ready at all times to be flashed. I feel so sad for the men who do that. No matter how many times I tell them I don't want to see it, they just love showing it. Is it because we are in the times of instant gratification and pictures? Most of the time it's a two out of ten anyways and how in the world can I meet them for coffee after trying to erase that image out of my eyes!? I've met men with completely fake pictures and names and a wife at home. Then, there's Hinge. I tried it once and the guys seemed a bit better in their careers. However, unless you pay you may only swipe five guys a day. I found it to be unsuccessful and quit. Tinder...oh, Tinder. It definitely has a reputation of being a "hook up" app. But, when I tried it I realized all the same single men are on every single app. Poor us single people. All looking for friends with benefits or friends or hookups or some like me...looking for our one true love, second time around. Bumble is fun because the woman makes the first move to talk, but it is exhausting. I find it a great time filler when I am lonely, however, I am not one of the lucky ones who has found anything to last after I don't send sexy pics or I just get ignored down the line and I guess I feel like I deserve someone who cares how my day is every day. So, I delete and try to be happy by myself and get closer to God. Then, I shake my head at me and get back on.

Men, listen up because I will repeat this for you again. Women that are of any substantial value or who have self-worth do not want to see your d-pics. I know y'all are visual, but it is like being flashed and completely ruins the mystery and dreams we want to learn about you, so that we can fall in love with you. Every time I get one my first thought is "who else has gotten that garbage and this didn't work for them?" I get it that we are instantly gratified in technology and y'all like it from us, but it will mean more for you if you want a real, classy, wifey material woman who doesn't want to see a picture of a penis. Men are born to chase. Women are born to nurture. I would rather see you in a sweater and nice sexy skinny jeans with a belt and imagine the smell of your neck than a sea animal that I cannot erase from my mind. I've even had men try to turn it back on me, knowing I am an empath by saying it hurts THEIR feelings that I don't like to look at their body. I also know there are girls out there that ask for it or send nudes. When I was very broken, I would send a sexy pic or two (to put it kindly) to get the feedback I needed at the time to feel better about myself. Then, I felt guilty for being so trusting. I would joke around and say "the ultimate sign of trust in a relationship is sending nudes with your face in it". On the flip side, I heard a piece of advice once for someone who felt unsexy and overweight. It was just a meme, but it said something about "Have you ever gotten naked in front of a man and he said 'no thank you'?" And most women should answer that with a no. I have, however, met men who have told me stories of, literally, escaping a naked desperate woman chasing them screaming "Do you want this?!" Why is it that we women feel so insecure that we use our beautiful bodies as a tool to gauge our own self-worth to a man who should love us for the person we are...then we don't even get to know who they really are because we blind them with sexual bait? Then get mad when they don't even know what to do except flash us back?

It is OK to get on and off dating apps. I find it very overwhelming and at times difficult to talk to multiple men at the same time. I am a one woman man, however, I will not settle. Sometimes being off the dating apps is when I have had to force myself to just relax and be comfortable hanging out with me. It really is a journey into loving yourself. When you are ready, it's OK to get back on the dating horse and try again. But, knowing yourself and not seeking a man to fill a void in your life is key. If I go on a date now, I know right away that it isn't going to work out, and if it is worth it, I friend zone until proven otherwise. I am OK keeping friends with some of them, but my time is valuable and sometimes it isn't worth the free meal to be in bad company, even for an hour. My favorite line to tell myself over and over is "Lean Back!" I literally make up songs and look at myself in the mirror at times and say "Lean Back Tiffany!" I think at one point I thought it was my personal mission to date and find that instant love. Someone reminded me that a tree does not bear fruit overnight. Leaning back and listening to your gut and looking at the situations with clear eyes will enable the true person to show. They say the first three to four months is the "infatuation" phase. Nobody has made it past that for me or for them. Some have stayed dear friends. Some have been blocked and deleted. If it is meant to be, won't it just be anyways?

Lean back. Lean back. Lean back. Lean back and never attack! (high kick)! Lean back. Lean back. Lean back and (fill in the blank...don't touch my rack, never look back, jiggle your own sack, look at the facts...) From what I have seen, men do like to chase. However, I have seen men want the woman to tell them they like them and be assertive. I definitely do not have the answers or I would be in a relationship. However, for my own feministic approach, I want a man to want me properly. I have had guys be honest and tell me they are intimidated by me. I have seen guys chase girls that are playing them, using them, and cheating on them. Sometimes, I wonder if they would rather have a girl who is less than me because they are not willing to put in the effort or maybe my strength makes them feel weak. I have also had nice guys that are showering me with flowers and I feel absolutely suffocated and have to cut them like a queen saying "off with their heads!" which probably isn't the kindest thing to do, but there has to be a balance. I cannot force it and they shouldn't either. All I can do is trust God and know that when He feels I am ready, or maybe my future lover is ready, He will bring him to me and it will be exceedingly, abundantly more than I could ever imagine.

I have gone through so many times being so unbelievably lonely and miserable. I remember my dad telling me the waves of emotions post-divorce will still occur, just get less frequent. One day I will be sad, the next angry and bitter, and the next I am dancing around the kitchen feeling so happy to be free. I often question if I am trying too hard to find my dream man. I have good men that are friends with me that tell me "all the women on the apps just want to get married right away and it scares me." It's almost like it's making it nearly impossible to happen. When I try, I get burned. I don't know why God wants me to be single. My ex and his girlfriend shoving their traveling and money in my face at any opportunity they can. What is God trying to teach me? Why am I so obsessed with finding my soulmate? Why can't I just be content all the time?

On the flip-side, so many of us experience break ups and sadness after either deciding to leave a toxic relationship or getting our hearts broken. I have helped so many of my close friends on how to move on and BLOCK. One thing I find myself telling them over and over again is "you have to block to heal". Think about it, you only remember the best of times from that relationship. You are so focused on what highs or what could have beens and it is so hard to let go sometimes. How can you begin to love yourself and, literally, force yourself to move on and heal if you do not cut that soul tie off? I guess, sometimes, I just feel like if I do not delete the number from my phone and truly block them on all avenues, how will I ever begin to heal and sometimes protect myself from further pain that I would rather choose to NOT know than to deal with more heartache? You have to almost rehab yourself into forcing the boot camp of loving yourself more than to choose someone who is not loving you properly. Sure, sometimes it does take forgiveness and grace, but other times it takes so much joy out of you that the only option you have left is to block. You can still pray for them and again, choose to love yourself more.

There is a fine line between love-bombing and love-at-first-sight. I haven't been very good at determining the difference. But, my gut is guiding me and I don't mind waiting to see who someone is in time. I have no problem identifying red flags and blocking in order to protect myself. I have had complete panic attacks when starting to fall for someone and it always ends up to be the wrong thing. I have read so much about masculine/feminine energy and making a man chase me and I started to think I believe none of it. I read that I should go weeks without responding to him to make him chase me. I can't go twenty-four hours. No human has the answer to finding love. Love that lasts and just comes easily.

"Love is patient, love is kind. It does not envy, it does not boast, it is not proud. It does not dishonor others, it is not self-seeking, it is not easily angered, it keeps no record of wrongs. Love does not delight in evil but rejoices with the truth. It always protects, always trusts, always hopes, always preserves. Love never fails. But where there are prophecies, they will cease; where there are tongues, they will be stilled; where there is knowledge, it will pass away."

1 Corinthians 13:4-8 New International Version

Maybe God is trying to use me for a reason that I don't know yet. Maybe being so open and willing to find love and still trying to cope with being forced into doing life alone, even as a beauty queen, and even through a pandemic, is so that everyone else that is single can see that it doesn't matter. Even a queen, with many men constantly trying to be in my life, I struggle. And, I will not settle. I would die alone if it meant avoiding someone who doesn't love me unconditionally. God, send me an angel of a man and I will make him the happiest man in the world. I will wait for it.

"Mr. FWB" (friend with benefits):

As I sat back, I had a realization. There is a man I met online almost a year ago that has been here all along. He has been a friend and we have talked and video chatted almost every day for eleven months. During all the crazy quarantines and the ups and downs of my dating drama, he was always there to talk. He has liked and commented on almost everything I post on my social media. He has opened up to me and we have even prayed for each other. When we finally spent time together I felt like I was with my best friend and I could just listen to him talk and laugh all day. He loves his family, friends and his amazingly perfect pup. He was always respectful when I would tell him I was seeing someone and there for me to talk to when it didn't work out. He is handsome and hardworking and MAN. He is the first man I have zero anxiety about. He has shared so much of his heart with me and I know he just wants a family and deserves affection and love and to not always be the single one of everyone he knows. Sometimes I stare at him and my mind just says "he is so cool" and I just want to be with him and make sure he is happy at all times. I will continue to stay on the path of my goals and he will, hopefully, just be by my side because I can't imagine not having him in my life, even if we just stay good friends. I have cried and begged God to send me my other half and prayed for my future soulmate. Has he been here this whole time? Building trust and supporting me while I chased people who were completely wrong for me? Could he be my Mr.? Could he love me as much as I love him? I picture us retiring together. I know he wants a family and I could still have children. I also know he looks at me in that way that I just smile and blush and although he doesn't know it, I feel like I can read his mind. I will continue to let him lead and proceed in my feminine and focused way. I will not fear the future with him because he wouldn't hurt me and I don't need to try to test or self-sabotage him. We have so much fun when we do literally anything. I am excited to see what happens next and just want us to keep living our lives supporting each other and laughing and holding hands for now. I can go through the dream man checklist and he has the ability to check off all of them and more. Time will tell. My focus is to just continue to love myself. I only die once, so I just choose to spend time with people who make me happy and he makes me happy. It is nice to have no pressure and just have someone to spend time with and laugh. He will always be my friend, but if he is meant to be my lover, time will tell. No eggs in any baskets.

Update...he just wants to use me. I started developing real feelings and he told me "I don't want to commit". WTF does that mean? Like, you want to date other people and use me as a girlfriend front? You think you know someone after a year, but apparently he is just like everyone else who is on dating apps trying to experience every kind of woman they can before they die. He even cried to me that his fear is to die alone.

Another update...He just posted he is "In a relationship" on Facebook! OMG! Good luck with that and thanks for the memories!

Off the apps again I go. Time to focus and release. I think I am finally to the point of letting it go. I have so much to look forward to and so much to offer. I will stay friends with anyone who wants my friendship and values my time and I enjoy being around. The rest is just fine because I am happier alone loving myself and feeling no pain than chasing someone who doesn't deserve me.

Dating takes courage. Dating takes putting on your best clothing, best shoes and perfume, shaving your legs and walking in with optimism and confidence, even when you are scared. Almost like a pageant. Maybe it's already rigged and the heart of the judge is already with another candidate. Maybe the judge will choose you, but then wants to own you and destroy you if you don't like something they do to you while representing you. I will tell you, queen, we are worth being our own judges. All we can do is be open and open our hearts, minds, ears, mouths and hands. However, we will not just choose anyone to be our king. Our King, God, is the only one who knows who is perfect for us and He will bring us our perfect partner when He feels we are ready. Sometimes, I think God is telling me, "Stop telling me what to do, Tiffany." But...LOL I think God is giggling and so am I.

MY DREAM MAN

This is my list I have been working on for four years. I reference it often. These are my non-negotiables and I suggest making one of your own (we will get there later in this book). Note: these are not in order of importance in any way.

- Loves and believes in God and will pray for me and our family and wants to be with me even after we die, in eternity.
- Goal oriented
- Handy
- Gives back, good reputation in the community he serves
- Best friend
- Funny
- Knows what he wants
- Protective
- Handsome (takes care of his appearance)
- Talented at his passion or hobby or craft
- Not hiding anything i.e. phone or social media or secrets
- No shirtless selfies online, on social media or to other women besides me
- No dick pics!
- Sexual connection and trust intimately
- A good parent if he has children
- Will have fun trying new things with me and I will try new things with him
- Financially stable and plans for the future

- Talks out our issues or takes a break then we talk it out/lets me take a break when needed
- Doesn't try to change who I am or compete with me
- Is proud of me
- Makes me feel like a teenager with him
- Travel partner
- Sees beauty in the little things
- Gives me compliments
- Tells me kindly when I am wrong
- Is willing to say I'm sorry too
- Honest
- Patient
- Trustworthy
- My family likes him and he likes my family and I like his and they like me
- Can agree to disagree and move on
- Loyalty
- Cuddles and touches, affectionate
- Wants to try fun date nights weekly, even if it costs nothing
- Opens his heart to me and tells me the hard truths he has inside

- Teaches me new things patiently
- Has short term and long term goals
- Consistently communicates and cares about what I am doing and lets me know what he is doing (not overly if he's busy but let's me know he's thinking of me and wants to make sure I am OK)
- Forgives me when I make a mistake and doesn't ignore me but wants to talk it out and fix it quickly...accepts my apologies how I would his.
- Makes me feel like I am the most beautiful person and like I am floating
- Loves me as much as I love him

Later in this book you will have a chance to explore your dream man checklist. What qualities are important to you? What are your non-negotiables? Even if it is physical or may seem silly to you, write it down and work on it often. Every single man I have met in my entire dating journey has been 100% different from each other and taught me new things to accept or determine to be something I will not stand for. Sure, nobody is perfect, but some things are worth waiting for, hoping for, praying for and dreaming to find. You deserve everything you want and more and so do I. All we can do is have faith and keep loving ourselves and others and wait. Like the queen I am, alone in my castle...I will wait.

YOU AS A BAD ASS BEAUTY

I knew every skincare, makeup and perfume at the department stores. I knew ingredients, price, and what customers liked and disliked. Traveling for work was fine, as long as I stayed clear of the married men who hit on me at the airports and hotels. I met so many amazing customers along the way. All seeking advice on how to look and feel their best. I learned how to explain the science behind beauty products and ingredients in relation to the skin. Then, how to choose the right makeup to enhance a woman's natural beauty based on their budget, if they even had one.

Let's take a look at skincare and what you need to know, from my experience. I am also in the process of developing my cosmetic line that is based on peach oil and I want to relay the benefits of it for your skin as I develop it and write this book. First of all, peach oil is found to be an elixir for bad moods and absent-mindedness. This is why I believe that it is what I want to base my line on for myself and others to use every day. I also know that there is an opportunity in every time you shower to reset your mind. Whether it is at the beginning or the end of the day. When you pray and meditate and talk to yourself in the shower it is your time. It is a time for you to be thankful for Holy water. I believe everything is made from God. Everything is everything from God! I try to focus on my blessings when I do my beauty routines and either set my day to see everything I look at as a blessing or put myself at a place of peace before I rest my head to sleep and wash negative thoughts and voices away.

Cleanse with mindfulness-

When you wash your face, morning or night, I want you to think of how you can turn it into an opportunity to meditate and pamper yourself. When you wash your forehead, I want you to tell yourself to wash away bad thoughts. Quiet that nasty inner-voice that tells you something is or could go wrong. Tell yourself a compliment of something you think or thought for yourself or others that day. If it is morning, clear your mind and prepare it by telling yourself you are smart and you will make only amazing choices today. When you wash your eyes, close them and erase anything bad you saw from them.

Choose to only "see" the blessings and miracles that are in your view. When you wash your ears and jaw, relax and choose to only hear the positive blessings that are said to you. Choose to open your ears to amazing advice so you can remember it. Choose to block out and erase any negative comments, gossiping, or put downs from the day or to prepare yourself for the day ahead. When you wash your nose, clean the grooves and pores around it, as to "smell the roses of life". Smell the fragrance or essential oils in the face wash and thank God that you have the money to afford a face wash. Wash your mouth. You will tell yourself to only say kind things and only speak words of encouragement to others.

Wash anything you said that day that didn't feel right and focus on how you can say the right things to fix it. Think of people in your day that you need to talk to, even if it's just to tell them you miss them, love them, appreciate them or are proud of them.

Cleansing your skin with the proper cleanser is important. Some cleansers are creamy, lotion-y, gel-like, exfoliating, no foam, or foaming. I really feel it is a personal preference. Avoiding something that is going to leave a residue or make you feel too dry is the key to finding what is best for you. When cleansing your skin, it is important to consider PH balance and not over-scrubbing. If you are oily, for example, sometimes you may think it is best to over clean. In turn, you are actually stripping too much of your skin's natural oils and your skin will overcompensate by producing extra oil, which causes bacteria to form and will lead to breakouts.

My dream face wash will have peach oil because it leaves the skin clean, no residue, not stripping, and removes makeup. It naturally cleans the pores and eliminates toxins. Even when washing your ears, peach oil aids in ear congestion and earaches.

Treat your perfectly made skin, your largest most active organ-

There are so many products to choose from! Where do you begin? I sold anti-aging creams that were $17-$1,500. Most people just want to know what is going to address their specific needs the most. From the time you are twenty-one, they say, the aging damage has already begun. From that point, it is trying to keep it from showing at the surface.

First, some people experience oiliness or acne. A lot of oily skin type folks refuse to use moisturizer because they hate the way it feels. Again, if you give your oily skin the hydration it is so thirsting for, it will not overproduce oil anymore which causes bacteria to form that will lead to breakouts. Sometimes people have extreme dryness. Some people start to then see uneven skin tone, dark spots, discolorations.

Not to mention..wrinkles, then sagging skin! AHHHH! I always said, some people are sinkers and some are saggers. Sinkers are losing the volume in their skin. Saggers are losing the elasticity and tightness. Think a raisin vs. a grape. Eeek. Why do you think grandma would pinch your cheeks and say, "Look at this face!"

There are three main causes of aging. First, is chronological aging. Birthdays, can't stop 'em!

Second, is hormonal aging..yikes.

Third, is environmental.

You know how when you cut an apple open it turns brown? That is called oxidation, or free-radical damage. It is happening to your skin every day, all day. Did you know peach oil is a natural antioxidant?

It eliminates the free radical damage that happens to our skin all day every day because it is packed with Vitamin E, B, C, and A. Those also help prevent hyperpigmentation. They help with psoriasis and eczema and help create healthy cell reproduction. They have linoec (for congested oily skin) and oleic fatty acids (for dryer skin). Peach oil contains Omega 3 and 6 which softens the skin, reduces irritation, acne, dryness, is anti-aging and balances the skin. It contains PUFA's (polyunsaturated fatty acids), which plumps out your wrinkles and tightens the loose rubber band-stretched out skin! And sinkers, it has Boron, which will give suppleness back to your cheeks that only grandma loved to pinch! It has calcium, magnesium, and potassium that boost the bridge that holds your skin firmly.

As you can see, there are many benefits to my dream peach product line I am working on developing. As a licensed cosmetologist and salon owner (you will find out more about that later in this book), the vitamins in peach oil also help with red blood cells that promote hair growth and heal your hair follicles. It also had Vitamin B7 which contains Biotin, and that will help a dry, damaged scalp and hair. So, I am also working on developing a shampoo and conditioning line. Also, peach oil restores nail surfaces and adds natural shine to your nails. So maybe a hand and foot cream would be necessary to create! Add a little shimmer instant body makeup glow to this and we can use it head to toe and just become yummy, glowing peaches ourselves!

No matter what you use, however, connect with each part of your body as you apply it. Be mindful of what you are doing to nourish the inside just as much as you pamper the outside. It is crucial for you to face yourself. As you take care of your beautiful outside, you will start to notice your features that you love about yourself. Put some music on that makes you feel like a happy or relaxed queen. Practice every day and don't ever stop.

And remember, you are as pretty as a peach!

PART 4:

"THE MS. MANIFESTO"

What is a Ms.?

THE PAGEANT WORLD

I only did one beauty pageant when I was about ten years old in Georgia. I was a complete brat and my mom told me she would never go through that again, haha! The day after I posted on Facebook that I was officially divorced, sitting in my amazing little cute apartment I received a phone call that would change my life forever. The head of the Illinois International Pageant system had been watching me and called me and said, "We are creating the first ever Ms. Illinois International and we would like to have you compete to represent that you don't need a 'king' to be a 'queen'. Now is the time. It is meant for you". I had literally just hung up with her when I received the call that the "other woman" that my ex dumped attempted suicide. I was, actually, crying for her. Again, he wasn't worth that. It broke my heart for my former best friend. Then, just like that, I was crying tears of joy minutes later at the thought of becoming the first ever Ms. Illinois International. I prayed for her. I talked to God a lot. He told me to do it.

Doing the pageant was the most exhilarating and brave thing I have ever done for myself aside from graduating from beauty school, buying my own home and opening an in-home salon, which all happened within a month of each other! It's amazing how much you can accomplish in a couple of years when someone isn't putting you down. My friends all came to support me and cheer for me and my son was standing with his arms raised screaming every time I stepped on that stage. To be honest, I could not even look at him for more than one second or I would burst into tears every time I stepped out. The inner voices and all the negative things my ex and his family used to say to me on a daily basis made me want to run to my car and quit every second of that pageant. Yet, the other girls were smiling and cheering for me and my son. My son was watching me face my fears and be strong and confident and go for a dream. He saw me when I thought I was broken into a million pieces and because of that director of the pageant, they put a crown on my head and told me I was important and special again.

It began, my daily reminder of what I am supposed to do. I am supposed to show people how to rise up from trauma. I am supposed to show my son and future family how to give back. I have been given this honor to not only gain my self-confidence, but to represent that when you feel like someone has thrown you away you are not garbage. Being Ms. Illinois International 2020 was not a time to dance with the Chicago Bulls dancers, be in a parade or two, or throw out an opening pitch at a Chicago Cubs game. It would have been, but there was a pandemic.

Of course, there is a stigma about pageants and I am here to tell you there is a wonderful side to the sport of pageantry. Being a queen has afforded me self-confidence to keep me motivated in accomplishing my hopes, wishes, and dreams. It is nothing like what people judge it to be as superficial as outer beauty alone. The opportunity to shine on stage again like I did when I was in high school has built me back up to being a powerful single female again. One who has an inner voice sparkling like my crown reminding me that I am special. I use it to help others in need, raise money and awareness for causes that are extremely important. Even when I am busy working and running my business and teaching e-learning and being a mother and running a household alone...I make time to give back. That is one different aspect of my parenting philosophy I want to show my son and what I want to be known for.

2020 was a year to safely help others in need. My platform, my charity, was to help victims of domestic violence and their children. During this pandemic the World Health Organization reported a 50-60% increase in the chances of women and children in the exposure of domestic violence according to the amount of calls from their hotlines. Isolation, financial stress, increased alcohol, and drug abuse are all increasing stress and the numbers of murder-suicides also increased. There were also men who reached out to me in the midst of their divorce hell with women who had affairs and/or falsified court documents and made false accusations against them. It makes me so angry when a woman accuses a man of abuse when it is not true. Luckily, I was able to guide some of them to much needed legal help and advice or support, too. If you want help or want to help someone that is a victim there are plenty of amazing resources and it is ok to seek help. My son and I have been spending our entire year, with many more to come, helping these victims and their children when they need it so badly. We help serve in any way possible and will hope to continue for the rest of our lives.

I went to Youtube a lot during the last few years. I watched a lot of Toni Robbins, "Real Talk Kim", who I was honored to meet and hug when she came to Chicago on my first post-divorce birthday and the amazing Pastor T.D. Jakes. I fell asleep many nights listening to them preach and it was therapy. I listened to them on my trips to court which were so scary. I cried and prayed and listened. T.D. Jakes said something I believe is real. He said, "When you as a parent hear your child cry, sometimes you let them because you know they need to learn. But you know the cry when you stop what you're doing and throw down whatever is in your hands and run to your child? That is what God does to you." I think I am finally done crying those cries that made God run to help me or send me an angel when I needed it so desperately sobbing on my knees. The stress of my divorce put me in the hospital eight times, alone, with unexplainable abscesses and the doctor finally found the cause was stress. Being alone in the hospital with no family around is something nobody should ever have to go through. Sometimes my ex-husband would be the only person able to drive me home after surgery and he would laugh at me. My son would see that and it led to tears and more pain and stress that took its toll on my body. I am grateful that I reached out to my doctor, therapist, personal trainer and pastors when I needed it. I got medication for my panic attacks and I used it responsibly until I didn't need it anymore. My friends and clients that came to me for their hair during beauty school and still, you all were my angels every single day. I will forever remember.

Whatever your pain is, what you go through in life, maybe it's your purpose. Maybe what makes you most angry or bothered is your calling to help fix or relieve others from. I cannot tell you how many people I know who have so much to give or be grateful for and do nothing. As a hair stylist I hear a lot, it's my job. In Illinois it is a requirement to take domestic violence certification courses for a reason. It is my goal to help anyone, male or female who experiences abuse, verbal, emotional, or physical to cope and heal and escape. Dealing with narcissists is another thing.

The book "Psychopath Free" by Jackson MacKenzie is an incredible resource. As an empath, it is normal to seek understanding of the why and the how these people think and behave towards others in the manner they do, because if you were one, you would never ask yourself if you were one.

I am truly an empathetic person. Empathy is defined as the ability to understand and share the feelings of another. (New Oxford American Dictionary). I have that. When someone shares with me anything they feel or go through, I have the blessing and curse to climb into the imagery they describe that I see in my head and truly feel what it would be like. My mom always tells me I cannot save every puppy. I always think in my mind "But I want to!!" There's a Wonder Woman quote from the movie that a dear friend of mine (angel) helped me learn how to turn it on and off.

"I used to want to save the world. To end war and bring peace to mankind, but then I glimpsed the darkness that lives within their light. I learned that inside every one of them there will always be both. The choice each must make for themselves—something no hero will ever defeat." -Diana, Wonder Woman movie

In other words, people have the choice and power to do anything they want, but they have to want it themselves. We can only control how we treat others and make them feel. If I ever made anyone feel bad, my goal would be to always pray for them and remind myself that I can put my head on my pillow every night and control only my actions. I will never quit trying to help others, however, some people must help themselves. If anyone ever feels hurt by me, I am sorry.

And yes, thanks to Covid-19 and salons being closed for a while, I decided to go back to my natural hair color... and I am channeling my inner Wonder Woman. The woman God made me to be.

Now, I am working towards my new goal. I applied for Ms. World International 2021 and I was selected to represent Illinois! I am going to compete on worldwide television and wear a bikini on the beach in Miami! At forty years old, it is my honor and privilege to get in the best shape of my life and stand tall and speak the truth of what it means to be a survivor of divorce and be a queen...by myself! Women from all around the world will be there representing their states and countries and I am honored to be representing mine. I hope this is an opportunity to share my story and my light with everyone. Whether I take home a crown or not, I am going for it! Stay tuned, Aug. 8-11, 2021 and filming for the reality show "Queen of the Crowned" will be my next step. If you are reading this after the pageant, you will already know if I won a title or not (there are many that will be given). No matter what happens, I am already a queen and will be excited just to explore this next courageous challenge!

Looking back at how far I have come post-divorce, I feel like it is not an end, but just the beginning. There's no telling where I will be in another year, or decade. The thought of everything I have been through and accomplished anyways, because there wasn't someone putting me down, is really astonishing. My son sees it. He is happy when he is with me and that is all I care about.

Like a queen, maybe even a Disney princess, all alone in my castle. Letting my hair grow like Rapunzel. No King. Finally learning that nobody needs to enter the castle. I am a prize. I am waiting for the right and perfect person. Someone who I build trust and friendship with. Learning to be content being alone and staying home and not trying is very difficult. Everyone tells me that is when it will come... when I stop trying so hard. Would Fiona from Shrek get on Bumble if she had a cell phone when she was in the tower alone? Every day I just keep leaning back and getting stronger. Of course, I am scared. I am afraid this book is putting my entire life out there and I could be a flop. I cannot quit, though. I am not a quitter and I love doing things that are scary and crazy and I only hope it inspires you to do the same, whatever your goals are.

COPARENTING, TWO YEARS LATER

As a mother of a young child, it is the single most heart wrenching thing to not be able to care for and watch over your child when you want to, which for me, was all the time. I felt like he was being taken away from me every week for those days and overnights. My parents are divorced. When I was two, my biological father cheated on my mother with..you guessed it..her next door neighbor best friend. History really did repeat itself. I don't remember much about him because he only visited once a year eventually which went to zero when I was about ten years old. I am truly blessed, however, to have the world's most amazing step-father who I call my dad. I feel like I am his baby girl. He is the kindest, smartest, hardest working, funny, trustworthy man I know. He is my rock alongside my mother. Knowing he is always there for me helps me sleep at night. He would do anything for my sister, brothers, and I. I acknowledge that not everyone is so fortunate and blessed. My ex hates my parents. His parents would make fun of me and tell me I was just like them. I was so confused because I love them. They were with me every step of the way during my divorce and nobody on Earth understood or worried more about me and felt my cries. Mom and Dad, thank you. I'm sorry if I ever felt like you weren't there for me. You were and I also can admit I was scared and sad and angry and bitter and confused..the waves you told me about that I would feel that are less and less as time goes on. I love you and I appreciate everything you have done to give me strength and faith in God because I could not have made it this far without it.

When I was missing my son during my divorce there was a long period of time that I will admit the minute he left I drank. A lot. I was in a hotel part-time those nights he had his parenting time, eventually, and I knew party time needed to be over because it was going to get me in trouble or extremely depressed. I can tell you the exact feeling the first night I spent a night alone in that hotel sober and proud of myself. I was Googling "how to deal with sadness coparenting," as I Googled a lot looking for advice and resources when I was going through my Hell. I found a story of a single mother of an infant. She was breastfeeding and had to pump enough storage to hand her baby over to her ex-husband and I found that to be terrifyingly worse. She said when she talked to God about it He said to her to rest and trust Him because she was coparenting with God. Since that day, I started to look at it as God giving me a little break. Time to let Him take care of my son so that I could take care of myself. I started to learn that it was OK to go out with friends, date carefully or just be alone and sing, read or write or color or binge Netflix!

Especially during Covid-19 quarantine. I couldn't even see my best friends. I learned how to love myself alone more than ever. I learned how to watch 4th of July fireworks on my patio and hug myself. I learned how to dance and sing karaoke by myself. I learned how to look in the mirror and say, "I love you, you beautiful, smart, kind loving bad ass woman!" and mean it.

My ex and I utilize a co-parenting app now. It is a game-changer. It has helped me to just communicate the important things and let go of any irrelevant gaslighting or pain. It documents everything and can be monitored and utilized in court, if needed. You cannot block your co-parenting ex, of course. So, if you are struggling I would highly recommend it.

It is such a struggle for this precious boy of mine, going from two completely different homes back and forth with two extremely different parenting styles. To say that he has to "adjust" when he comes back to me is an understatement. I can't imagine what that feels like. I just encourage him to keep going to counseling and have a neutral party to talk to. He wants to please us both. I just want him to know he can always count on me to give him a calm, clean, safe, happy and fun environment. I don't think all the vacations and elaborate toys and luxuries he lacks at my home matter as much as I worry about. I do have to clean his attitude towards me every week or he just cries to me as soon as I see him. Funny thing is, I still do that to my mom, too, sometimes when I break down at forty years old. To cook or color or watch a movie, bike ride or just dance I really think are our most special times for him. I tell him that he is blessed to have everything he could ever need and when he walks in my door he breathes a sigh of relief and is happy to be home. I watch for it and it happens every time.

TRAVELING ALONE!

The first time I planned a trip with my son, we were going to drive nine and a half hours to Tennessee to watch my Miss Illinois sister queen compete for Nationals. We stopped in Indiana to visit my grandparents' graves and I took a minute under my breath to talk to my grandmother and thank her for being an angel over me. I missed her. She used to tell me all the time how much Jesus loved me when I was upset or sad. I told my son about them and we talked to them and I feel like they finally got to meet him and visit him for the first time. We continued to Lexington, Kentucky, to stay overnight. The next day we visited a real castle and then Keeneland Racetrack. Seeing the racehorses practicing on the track was breathtaking.

I was very nervous driving so far and petting the hood of my car the whole time saying "Thank you God for my car not having problems" while contemplating the whole time what I would do if something broke or I was stranded on the side of the mountainous roads. We stopped at a hiking spot and I instantly regretted that goal. However, driving five miles up a mountain of curves and dangerous waterfalls, my son cheered me on to keep going! I was literally shaking. We got out and hiked. He pushed me to keep going. As we came down the hill I felt a sense of relief. I felt like stopping and sobbing and apologizing to my son for making him push me. I told him the struggle up the mountain for the past two years going through my divorce I could not have done without him by my side encouraging me to keep going. My son is growing up way too fast and I feel responsible. I made a promise to him, 'It is all downhill from here and he needs to just be a happy child because Mommy is better'. We made it to the hotel destination and had the best night and pool day the next day before the event. My sister queen won! We cheered and cried tears of joy for her.

A year later, I took a trip to Florida by myself for my fortieth birthday during Covid-19. It was a fabulous hidden gem of a resort that I had traveled to years ago when I was helping another territory training in my old job. Taking this giant leap of faith and traveling alone for the first time in my life answering to nobody whether I made it back from Starbucks, let alone the airport, was frightening and invigorating. It had been twelve years since my last vacation with my ex, which was an absolute nightmare. Sure, I have visited family and that was great, but this was an adventure because nobody was checking in on me. It had been a year of health fears, political fights and financial hardships for all. And it was my fortieth birthday! I have healed and cried and learned from this trip. I talked to God the whole time and looked at my beautiful ocean. I watched the sunrise and the sunsets alone.

I was obsessing over the Maya Angelou quote:

"You alone are enough."

I realized on this trip that I have never actually really been alone. I never really am alone. Is that what I and so many other divorced people are afraid of? Most women are not alone at age forty and when faced with divorce we all are coping with fears of loneliness. I have cried so many tears feeling sorry for myself. Yet, as I write these stories and even as I walk on the beach alone I am still in the presence of God, my family, my friends, the birds, the jellyfish, the dolphins, the marines on the ships in the distance keeping us safe, the Uber driver that I adored, the lady at the front desk who upgraded my room for me for my birthday, the bartender girls downstairs who I loved hanging out with, the people who are texting me, calling me, and cannot wait to see me again to see my joy and hear about this trip. If you just sit back and look, God sends angels and people and animals to us to remind us we are never really alone. I am not afraid of it anymore. I embrace it. I will lean back and take more adventures. I am excited and optimistic about the rest of my life. The first half is over. I have my son and I have my health and a lot of people who love me. And on top of it all, I love me and

I have my back like no other. I cannot wait to keep having fun with me and see what else I can learn! Watching the sunrise one morning, it hit me, just as the sun rises each day, we rise too and we have to shine so bright each day that we are given and see the other amazing people, places and things that the world has to offer. We just have to be open enough to focus our eyes on the beauty in all things we see.

I visited a local bar with a friend I met on the trip. Pete's Bar was apparently where John Grisham would go to write his books. I stayed seven days alone in that hotel and met friends and did even more healing. I worked on this book and thought about the journey. It was beautiful and I did it! Independence is a beautiful thing. I could go wherever I wanted, whenever I wanted. I could walk on the beach, get a massage, work out, take a nap, have a drink, order whatever food looked good to me, or even go on a date! Oh, wait! I can do that all the time! I am independent and I am happy!

MS. WORLD

So, you know that feeling when something comes popping into your head and makes you say, "No way, but maybe??" and you do it anyways taking all leaps of faith and putting aside all fears and doubts and doing it you think you're crazy, but you have to do it anyways? (my brain).

It was the beginning of a pandemic. Covid-19 was just entering the U.S. and we began a mind-boggling isolation. I had my amazing home so it didn't bother me to quarantine with my son and I kept my optimistic attitude. My salon eventually got shut down and I knew I had been writing and had dreams of publishing my book. Things were opening up in Wisconsin, so I took my son to the Dells. Immediately after the first day I started to feel sick. By the end of the trip I was so deep into fever, sore throat, and exhaustion and I had to get tested. It was positive. It was frightening, but mostly a mind game. Alone for fifteen days I figured I would just read back everything I wrote during my entire divorce and get writing again. When I read back the last words my former mother in law said to me, "We don't need or want you in our lives", it took me to a very dark place. I began to think that nobody needed or wanted me in their lives. I ended up getting another excruciating abscess "down there" which hadn't happened since the divorce stress. I Ubered myself to the ER and broke down so bad that the doctor was asking me if I needed mental assistance. I had emergency surgery and begged one of my best friends down the street to come pick me up. The doctor gave me the successful surgery report and told me I officially tested negative and beat Covid-19! Even though my neighbor friend (angel) was probably afraid to be in a hospital during this she was there when I came out of anesthesia. She drove me home and made sure I was in the house comfortably. I walked to my back patio and opened the blinds and the most brilliant rainbow I had ever seen was shining over my entire view. After I convinced her it was OK to go, I talked to God. As my favorite Pastor Kim says, "You have to be sick and tired of being sick and tired." I prayed and decided it was time to delete that book. A few days later, my next client in the salon was my former babysitter who still came to me for her hair and she prayed with me as we made sure it was gone from my trash and erased forever. We literally held hands and cried as every hair on my body was standing up. I immediately felt a sense of weight lifted off my chest like

I could breathe more clearly than I ever could. It was truly a release. I think I was holding onto the idea of writing a book, but that was not the story I wanted to tell. My mind had blocked so many memories for my own protection and I needed to not relive that in my mind ever again. I made a promise to myself that no matter what, I would not ever let my stress level or sadness ever get so broken again that I end up physically in the hospital. I stopped crying and I began to write this book.

I got a message in my DM's on Instagram from Ms. World International telling me I would be a great candidate for Illinois. I entered. And guess what? I got chosen for Illinois! So, here goes nothing. It is to be televised on reality TV. What am I doing?! I'm representing what it is to be a Ms. that's what! Even if I don't win, I can say I did it! So, I will continue this journey to see what happens. I will publish this book to hopefully inspire others to find who they want to be even after divorce or trauma. I will give back and show my son how to help others unselfishly. I will train my body to see how forty looks on me. I will also try to develop a skincare and cosmetics line based on peaches because they are amazing! I will keep making my clients feel beautiful on the outside while trying to heal their insides or make them smile. I will work hard and try not to have fears or self-doubt. I will travel and write about what I am learning so that if you are reading this you know that you are important and a queen too. If love comes my way, I will not settle for anything that pulls me down or back. I will make as many friends as possible and be loving and kind and I will listen. I may go back to school one day and become a paralegal, lawyer or a counselor. How can I use my healing and story of pain to help people get past divorce? Divorce is something that nothing can prepare you for. It is a break up, of course, but it is so unbelievably expensive and absolutely terrifying. It is your life, your heart, your money, your assets, your confidence, your children, your home, and your future, and it is all at risk.

On a complete other direction, I learned that all wild mustangs that are sent to auction are given a branding type stamp along the left side of their neck. It looks like this...

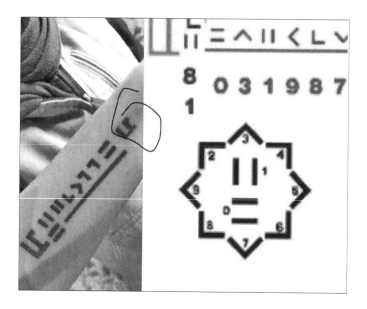

This is the owner's arm of one of my favorite horses named "On a Whim". She was named that because she was purchased on a whim. When a horse goes to auction they are allowed three times to be adopted or they are slaughtered. If you use the BLM decoder (Bureau of Land Management), The first U shape means she was born in the USA. The second is her birth year 10, or 2010. The rest that translates to 185440 means she is from California. I hope one day to get my own brand tattooed on my left side. Maybe one day when I get "adopted". Maybe with my birthday and my son's and my future family's.

Ironically, it is like when my biological father left me at a young age it was like I was adopted by my step-dad. The deep rooted feelings of rejection from a parent and then a husband made me feel at times I needed to seek a man to feel validated. However, I can now truly say I am of a different mindset. I no longer need to define myself by the way a man loves me or not because I am happy and content loving myself. Like "On a Whim" it will come to me and it will be incredible.

One day, as I accomplish all my individual goals, I will find my true love of a man. I want more children. Whether he has some too or I have more, I will be open to what God has in store for me. I am forty years old and I don't want to settle. I will continue my journey as a powerful Ms. as I set my personal affirmations and accomplish my goals. I will publish my book. I will be brave.

Day by day, the only thing I can do is focus on giving my heart and support and joy to everyone I see. I need to take in all the blessings that I have and see. I need to look in the mirror and love myself. God says we are supposed to trust Him. I am a queen of God and he will give me exceedingly, abundantly more than I can imagine, right? Sometimes, trusting God is the hardest thing to do and yet, having faith is our only option and the Bible tells us to. I pray for forgiveness for my mistakes. I am grateful for every single thing I have. Even sleeping alone in my bed is better than sleeping next to someone who doesn't treat me well. Looking back, I regret nothing. I would do it again because I have my son and I am rewriting what it means to have this last name until I may one day take another. My story is not over. It is just the beginning.

YOUR TURN

I think about the racehorses. This one in particular was featured on a race I happened to catch on TV, and I took these photos.

I was so scared on the left. My son could feel it. It was one of the few hours I wasn't crying in the midst of my Hell, on Mother/Son night at his school. On the left he is in kindergarten. On the right he is in third grade. Three years later...same time. My son, he is my champion.

So what do you need to do QUEEN? How do you rise up? How do you not give up? How are you going to rewrite your future? You have a second chance at the rest of your life. You can do this...you are not alone ever and you are perfectly made. For us all, we will experience trauma at some point in our lives. It has already been written, but the decision is yours and yours alone. We just need to take the time each day to look in the mirror and say, "I love you". We need to start telling ourselves to wash away the negative thoughts and clear our minds, ears, eyes, mouths, and convince ourselves each and every day to focus our conscious thoughts on the angels around us that God shows us and be grateful for each gift we are given. You are an angel, too. What will your journey look like in three years? Ten? Sixty? You are not defined by what happened TO you. What will you do with it?

What is the situation that happened TO you?_____

_____

_____

What was it that you did that you feel like you did by mistake? Why?_____

_____

How can you release it and finally forgive yourself? Ask God for forgiveness? If so, write your prayer here. Guess what? God forgives you. _____

_____

_____

What dreams do you have that you can revisit or want to try now? _____

_____

What is standing in the way? _____

_____

What can you do about it? Who can you reach out to for help?

_____

_____

1 year plan _____

3 year plan _____

5 year plan _____

10 year plan _____

___ year plan _____

What makes you so amazing, QUEEN? _____

_____

What is your "Why"? _____

_____

How can you use this to help others? Is there a charity you
would want to help? _____

_____

_____

Write your prayer here:

_____

_____

_____

_____

_____

_____

_____

_____

_____

_____

_____

Make your Dream Man non-negotiable checklist here. Add
to it often and don't you dare settle:

_____

_____

_____

_____

_____

_____

_____

_____

_____

_____

_____

LOVE, MS.

Thank you for reading my story. You know the question, "If you could go back in time and tell yourself the things you know now, what would you say to yourself?" Well, let's dive into that. Because, dear, this is your new start to the rest of your life.

Dear Miss,

Princess, you are young. You have no idea how big the world really is (even though you think you do). You have so many ups and downs and changes coming your way. You can be anything you want to be and grow and change your story often at any time of your life in the future. Right now, though, you need to only focus on yourself, your dreams and create a path to your future..

There is this thing called a credit score (think of it like a grade in school that reflects how good your credit history is—850 is a perfect "A" and 450 is, well, let's just say you'll need to retake the final!) and credit cards (these guys are sneaky; bulk them up and you've got a problem). Both can affect your financial future. Young Miss, you need to protect your hard-earned money and keep working hard. No matter what dream boy comes your way, just worry about yourself right now.

Imagine working your heart out and one day as an adult having everything taken from you. I know you think he may love you, but he will change and so will you, a lot, you and he are different humans. I know dating and boys are fun and will always be fun, but just let it be that...fun. There is no rule that says you have to find your husband before thirty or have kids by thirty-two just because everyone else is doing it. No matter what your friends are doing or your family says is normal, just worry about yourself right now.

If he is the right person for you, it will be always and forever anyways. If there are problems early on with cheating, porn addiction, drugs, mental abuse...these are called "RED FLAGS". My mom told me once: "Whatever you like most about him in the first two months is what will piss you off about him the rest of your life". Also, "Whatever bothers you about him or what you fight about, multiply by 1,000,000,000 when you're married". I am not trying to scare you, young queen. I am trying to tell you to stop stressing about what fairy tales taught you about prince charming and your path, but hold onto them. Your path is different from anyone else's in the entire world. Get established, get strong, get a healthy bank account, get a stable career for now (it could change as things happen to you and you find new passions to use your strengths for). No matter the pressure our culture pushes on you to make a move before you're ready, just worry about yourself right now.

I always wanted to write a book and I have written two different ones in my past and deleted both of them because of self-doubt. Here I am, at forty, publishing a book and running for Ms. World. Alone. I shine now like the little girl who had her light put out for someone else's benefit. Shine, Princess, shine for you and only you! Let people love you. Do things for your community and society. Figure out how to make a difference. Don't let dating get in the way of finding who you are, who you are going to strive to be. Learn and exercise. Be responsible with money, your education, and your health. That is your only goal right now. Just enjoy being happy. No matter what the world wants from you, just worry about yourself right now.

Miss, you are doing amazing. You are on your way to a fantastic future. Maybe you are afraid of living paycheck to paycheck. It is NORMAL! You are getting smarter every day. You are beautiful. You will work hard, have your own place and maybe life wants you to move around locations to see the big world a bit. You don't need to cling to someone unless they are your EQUAL. As influencer and author, Ace Metaphor says, "2 times 0 is 0. 2 times 1 is still 2. But, 2 times 2 is 4. Wait for your equal." Do not stop until you are at that place of where you are nearing your place of contentment. Love really is blind. Listen to your gut. Listen to your friends and family. Ask them questions often. They aren't jealous or competing with you. These are the people who you will have forever, they love you unconditionally and they don't want to be wiping your tears again at age forty, fifty, sixty, they want you to be happy and they are your angels.

You care way too much about what other people think. However, you don't listen when the people who really love you see you making a mistake and try to baby step or tiptoe to tell you you're wrong if you are and they don't want you to be mad at them. Men can have complete midlife crises, and I have yet to meet a man who hasn't. They have issues with sex drive and testosterone and sometimes they feed their insecurities by destroying your light or flirting and having relationships behind your back. You probably know all about dating apps. It is scary and from what I have seen, men of all ages are on them all and some still in other relationships. Do you want to be married and play secret spy on him when his phone lights up next to his bed at night? Does he really give you all access to his entire life? Do not brush issues under the rug. You are incredible, smart, talented, beautiful, and worth waiting for and being heard. Nobody is perfect, but if you think to yourself "I would never do that to him" then you're right and it isn't okay. No matter how badly you want to "fix" things, just worry about yourself right now.

Maybe now just isn't the right time. Be safe, be smart, guard your money, and your beautiful heart. You aren't even half way through your life and things can change in an instant. Gain more experience and knowledge and travel and see the world. If you want a partner to do it with you, great! Enjoy every moment and grow with your best friend. Build an undeniable love and trust and openness that you know 100% with everything in you will last for the rest of your life until y'all are buried in graves next to each other holding hands under the ground. Isn't it ironic that all you care about is what everyone else thinks, yet you don't listen to what everyone else thinks? Please ask questions and trust your angels.

No matter what, just worry about yourself right now.

Love,

Ms.

Dear Mrs.,

I am so happy for you. You are married to your best friend and partner and you made the promise in front of God and everyone you love to cherish that partner for the rest of your life 'till death do y'all part'. I hope and pray you and he have everything you ever dreamed of. I hope you were so smart that people like me can look at you and what you have and really know you found your true love and soul mate and it gives us hope that true everlasting love is attainable. Please do not ever take his love for granted. Please do not ever make him feel emasculated and unappreciated. If you have children, you will be so unbelievably exhausted. Take note of the times he is trying to help you and doesn't understand you...because he isn't you and you aren't him. He wasn't trained on diaper changing and rocking babies. He has the weight of managing and protecting your home, your future, your family, and your safety on his shoulders and he probably beats himself up because it is his reflection of his capabilities as a "MAN".

If I ever get married and become a Mrs. again, I promise that I will never take for granted what my spouse does to support us or our family. I will not put him down or belittle him. I will never cheat on him. I will be financially responsible. If I make these vows to him I will keep my promise for the rest of our lives. If he has children I will not disrespect their mother if she is involved in their lives. I will love them like my own and treat them like the princes and princesses they are. I will carry my weight and contribute. I want to retire with him and live on a lake in the South and fish and listen to music and laugh with him. I want us to kiss, hold hands and make each other smile while we watch our children succeed. I will be there for him when he needs me, in sickness, and in health. He will never be alone...I will respectfully give him time of peace if he needs it though, whether with his friends or to unwind. I will give him the trust he gives to me.

From what I have seen on TV and in real life, there are men who get extreme urges to cheat or have emotional affairs, especially at the midlife crisis time. Mrs., if you can make it through that, I want to know your secret because that is incredible! I have asked my "happily married" clients in the salon. Only the ones who have strong Christian foundations or have forgiven their partners for slightly or completely swaying have lasted, just from what I have seen. I'm a hairdresser...I hear a lot. However, my female clients do have affairs, too. Maybe they have an old high school crush that says, "Hello, beautiful" in their DM's on Facebook. It feels good to know they still say, "You're beautiful". Maybe it's the man who loses his testosterone and some other woman makes him feel his urges again. All I know is I pray for you, Mrs. I pray you never have to experience the fear and worry of snooping on his phone late at night. I pray you and your husband have the magical love story that I always dreamed of...dying and being buried hand in hand. I pray you are the almost half of marriages that work out to last forever. I pray that you cherish and appreciate that man who is good to you. If you are not happy, and you gave it everything inside you, and you are not showing your children or yourself the love you deserve to feel, it is OK. It is so hard to let go, but you will get through it. God will send you angels and if you talk to Him, he will guide you. Fight for your family, but always fight for yourself. God bless all the happily married couples!

With great love for you and your well-being,

Ms.

Dear Ms.,

You are here!

Did you lose the love of your life? Did you want to? Did you ever see this as your future...when you walked down the aisle? Maybe you still haven't found the love of your life. As I think of every scenario possible that led you to being a Ms., I can 100% guarantee that the answer is no, you never wanted this. If you are a widow, I am so sorry and that is something I know nothing about. I cannot even begin to imagine how that might feel. But, if you are divorced or divorcing, this is for you. I know you never expected this trauma. I know you had a vision in your mind of what your future would look like and it has completely been your vision since you were a little princess. (At this point I am totally projecting, these are things I need to remind myself of every single "single" day).

Maybe you never got married and have been a Miss your whole life and are still single at fifty. Either way, Ms., you have only you to protect, support, love and comfort you. If you're like me, you may also have children that you are responsible for and play "mommy" and "daddy" at the same time on top of it. I know this isn't what little princesses were trained or taught to do. That is why you are here in the first place. How do we every day, alone, feel safe? How do we every day, alone, feel beautiful? How do we, alone, every day feel supported? How do we, every day, alone, feel loved? We have Faith in God as our King. We learn to accept the facts that this is reality. We put a crown on our own heads and tell ourselves anything and everything we don't hear from a partner. We fight, we work, we push through because the pain we are going through, each and every one of the pains...is to help another. Maybe it's a stranger, a friend, one of our children who are watching. Most of all, remember this . . .

It is written. Don't you ever forget you are a queen. I love you.

Love,

Ms.

Afterword

At the time of this writing, I am soaring with my gown and crown to Miami, Florida to compete for Ms. World International. I am going to ride a horse again. I am in development of my dreamy and oh so peachy cosmetics line. I am putting all the trust into God's hands and the angels' hands that will be with me. I don't know which one scares me more...but I will work hard and watch the miracles happen!

Keep making your goals, too, queen! Don't be afraid.... Just LIVE YOUR LIFE in all that you do.

And waiting for the dream man? It will just have to come to me. No rush. :)

Where will life take me next? Here goes everything...
Crowns UP!!

Ask for Help

Emotional abuse is abuse. Extreme criticism, shaming, threats, and control are all still forms of domestic violence. Just because the bruise is on the outside, the ones on the inside are sometimes harder to aid. Abuse can be sexual, physical, emotional, or neglect. If you or someone you know is a victim here are some ways to get help;

- 911
- Domestic Violence Hotline 1-877-TO END DV or 1-800-799-SAFE (7233)
- Childhelp National Child Abuse Hotline
- Call or Text 1-800-422-4453 (1-800-4-A-CHILD)
- Live chat www.childhelphotline.org
- Crisis Counselor crisistextline.org or
- Text 741741 US and Canada
- Text 85258 UK
- Text 50808 Ireland
- www.kidshelpline.com.au in Australia
- Youth in trouble/Runaways 1-800-RUNAWAY (1-800-786-2929)
- National Suicide Prevention Lifeline 1-800-273-TALK (8255)
- National Parent Helpline 1-855-4APARENT (1-855-427-2736) 10am-7pm EST

Biography / About the Author

Tiffany Kory, author of "Ms." is exploring the journey of her life while rising up post-divorce as a single mother who is a beauty queen with no king. Growing up a southern belle, moving north, where time moves faster, she has become a successful salon owner and was crowned the first ever "Ms. Illinois International 2020" and now is reaching for the stars as "Ms. Illinois World International 2021" preparing to compete for "Ms. World International".

Throughout her life, she has learned how to love herself and was always aware of who she was, even in her younger years, with aspirations for her dreams to come true and to see now, the challenges that she has conquered. Ms. Kory is compelled to share her story with others to circumvent turning her pain into her purpose. She navigates this new beginning at forty years old as a risk-taker with an open book aptitude to advise on divorce, dating, independence, self-love, and self-care. With over twenty years of experience in the makeup and hair industry, she dedicates her life to helping others feel beautiful on the inside and outside.

Her inspiration is her son. Her dedication to supporting him and teaching him to bless others is what motivates her. And her strength to rise from trauma is to never let him feel like he cannot do anything he wants to do in his life.

She also wants you to own your title in the stage of your life. Whether you are a Miss or Mrs. or Ms. she wants you to know that you ARE never and WILL never... be truly alone.